Clement Boulton Roylance Kent

Essays in Politics

Wherein Some of the Political Questions of the Day are Reviewed from a

Constitutional and Historical Standpoint

Clement Boulton Roylance Kent

Essays in Politics
Wherein Some of the Political Questions of the Day are Reviewed from a Constitutional and Historical Standpoint

ISBN/EAN: 9783337234355

Printed in Europe, USA, Canada, Australia, Japan

Cover: Foto ©Suzi / pixelio.de

More available books at **www.hansebooks.com**

ESSAYS IN POLITICS

WHEREIN

SOME OF THE POLITICAL QUESTIONS
OF THE DAY ARE REVIEWED
FROM A CONSTITUTIONAL AND HISTORICAL
STANDPOINT

BY

C. B. ROYLANCE KENT, M.A.

LATE EXHIBITIONER OF TRINITY COLLEGE, OXFORD, AND LEE PRIZEMAN OF
GRAY'S INN, BARRISTER-AT-LAW

LONDON

KEGAN PAUL, TRENCH, TRÜBNER & CO., Lᴛᴰ.

1891

PREFACE.

THE word "Politics" may be used in two senses. It may be used in the wide, or what I may call the Aristotelian sense, as including all those questions which affect the life of men, as members of society; or it may be used in the narrower and somewhat debased sense, as including only those questions which happen for the moment to agitate the different parties in the state. It is in the former sense that I have used the word in the title of this volume. My aim, however, has been practical. I have attempted to consider some of the more important questions of modern politics from a constitutional and historical standpoint, and to give them their due place in the larger sphere or area of the political science to which they belong. "No perfect discovery," says Lord Bacon, "can be made upon a flat or a level; neither is it possible to discover the more remote and deeper parts of any science, if you stand upon the level of the science, and ascend not to a higher science." And

a 3

so in practical politics, in order to come to any right conclusion whatever, it is necessary to leave the flat or level of party controversy, and ascend to a higher standpoint. Never at any time was this more necessary than at the present moment. Some of the questions that the electors are now called upon, or will soon be called upon to decide at the polls, are of the highest importance, and go directly to questions of principle. Some, such as Irish Home Rule and Imperial Federation, are constitutional questions which can only be rightly considered when looked at as parts of the great subjects of sovereignty and federal government. Others involve the consideration of such weighty matters as the sphere and duties of government. Such is the now important question of the hours of labour. Others, again, involve a consideration of the nature and logical consequences of democracy. There must be many who, having been compelled "to embark into a troubled sea of noises and hoarse disputes, put from beholding the bright countenance of truth in the quiet and still air of delightful studies," will be called upon to form an opinion on these questions. These will have neither the time, nor perhaps the inclination, to seek for themselves facts and authorities, which are widely scattered and not easily accessible. It is for these at least, I hope, that the facts and arguments which I have collected, and which I have decked in as fair a literary dress as the subject and my own power have permitted, may prove of some use. I can make little or no claim for originality; indeed, in many cases I have been careful to name my authority. My aim has been throughout rather to state cases than to take sides. Lord Houghton is said to have remarked of Mr. Gladstone that his method of impartiality was being furiously in earnest on both sides of a question. I have tried to be impartial, but my way has been rather to state facts and arguments on both sides, and to draw only the most obvious inferences without prejudice and without passion.

In conclusion, I must thank the Editor of the *Westminster Review* for kindly permitting me to reprint the essay on the Progress of the "Masses" which appeared in November, 1887, and to rewrite an article on Federal Government which appeared in May, 1888, and which forms the basis of the essay on Federal Government in this volume.

C. B. R. KENT.

LIVERPOOL,
 March, 1891.

CONTENTS.

———•◦•———

ESSAY I.

SOME QUESTIONS OF SOVEREIGNTY.

ESSAY II.

FEDERAL GOVERNMENT.

ESSAY III.

THE POLITICAL INSTITUTIONS OF SWITZERLAND.

ESSAYS IN POLITICS.

I.

SOME QUESTIONS OF SOVEREIGNTY.

"THERE is also a doubt as to what is to be the supreme power in the state. Is it the multitude? or the wealthy? or the good? or the one best man? or a tyrant?" This suggestive and far-reaching question was asked long ago by Aristotle, and, in asking it, he opened up one of those interesting fields of inquiry which have justly earned for him the name of the father of the Science of Politics. The question here raised is one of capital importance in political science, and one which from the time of Aristotle to our own, has been the source of much discussion, and which even now cannot be said to be finally settled. It is nothing less than the question of sovereignty. What is the sovereign body? And where is it to be found in any given political community? These are the two branches into which the inquiry divides itself. No question probably has more occupied the minds of political philosophers. At all periods of history,

B

when any literature in political science has been produced at all, this question has been almost always
discussed. In the Middle Ages, indeed, writers were
either like Thomas Aquinas, or Dante, too much
occupied with arguing the claims of the temporal or
spiritual powers, or like Machiavelli, too much involved
in working out the details of practical statecraft, to
give much attention to it. But afterwards it was
always given a prominent place. Jean Bodin, a French
lawyer of the sixteenth century, was the first to give
anything like an adequate definition of a sovereign
body, when he wrote that it is limited neither by a
greater power, nor by any laws, nor by time, and that
the prince and people in whom sovereignty resides
are not answerable for their acts to any one except
immortal God. Sir Thomas Smith, who wrote shortly
after Bodin, defined sovereignty in a very similar
manner, but he differs from him in fixing its place in
Parliament. "And to be short," he says, "all that
even the people of Rome might do, either Centuriatis
Comitiis or Tributis, the same may be done by the
Parliament of England, which representeth and hath
the power of the whole realm, both the head and body."
Next it is very fully treated by Hobbes, who has the
great merit of being the first to distinguish policy
from legality, that is to say, what is expedient from
what is legally allowed. Closely connected with this
is the distinction between legal and political sovereignty, of which more will be said hereafter—a distinction which is of great importance, and which, if
not properly grasped, is fruitful in confusion and

misunderstanding. Even Hobbes himself is too much impressed with legal sovereignty to always keep it distinct. He sometimes himself falls into the mistake which he has pointed out to others. But nothing can be clearer than his conception of a legally sovereign body. He imagined, without any warrant it must be confessed, the existence of a person or body of persons invested by contract with the power of the whole community, and then he went on to say that "he that carrieth this person is called sovereign, and hath sovereign power, and every one besides is his subject." These are words of luminous clearness for that age, though in these days they seem simple enough. The next writer of importance after Hobbes is Locke. But just as Hobbes gave too prominent a place to legality, so on the other hand Locke gave too prominent a place to policy. But how clear his ideas of sovereignty were may be judged from the following sentence, where he said that "whilst the government subsists, the legislative is the supreme power, for what can give laws to another must needs be superior to him." Next in point of time comes Rousseau, who was so blinded by his inflated notions of the sovereignty of the people as to declare that there is no sovereign body in the state at all. After such insensate ebullitions as this, it is refreshing to turn to Blackstone, who defined sovereignty with all the precision of a lawyer. In all forms of government, he said, "there is and must be a superior, irresistible, absolute, uncontrolled authority, in which the jura summa imperii, or the rights of sovereignty, reside." The existence of a sovereign body, which

Rousseau denied altogether, he makes the very corner-stone of all political societies. Bentham, again, un-sparing though he was in his criticism of Blackstone, agreed with him in seeing the necessity of forming a clear conception of sovereignty. But this occupied a quite secondary place in his work, which was to demonstrate the purposes for which government exists, and the methods by which it might best attain its ends. Lastly, Austin, in his "Province of Juris-prudence Determined," has defined sovereignty in a manner that has laid for all time a sure foundation for the science of positive law.

This short historical sketch will be enough to show how large a space questions of sovereignty have occupied in the writings of political philosophers, and how important a branch of the science of politics it is. So important is it, that it is impossible to avoid confusions and escape inaccuracies without having first obtained a clear idea of its nature. And even when a satisfactory definition has been reached, it will be found that this is not all, but that many questions arise in connection with it, although it may well have been thought that all questions of sovereignty had been by this time finally settled. But this is very far from being the case, and it is some of these unsettled questions of internal sovereignty, apart from those questions of external sovereignty belonging to the sphere of International Law, which it is proposed to treat of here.

One of the first questions that arise is, Does there really exist, in certain political communities, any sovereign body at all? It will be found that there are certain political communities where it is very difficult to say whether there is really any actually existing sovereign body, and, further, when it has been found to exist, whereabouts in the community it lies. In order to determine these questions correctly, it is absolutely necessary to bear well in mind a clear definition of sovereignty. The best definition is Austin's; it is so good that no better could probably be framed. He says, "If a determinate human superior, not in the habit of obedience to a like superior, receive habitual obedience from the bulk of a given society, that determinate superior is sovereign in that society, and the society, including the superior, is a society political and independent;" and further, "to that determinate superior the other members of the society are subject, or on that determinate superior the other members of the society are dependent. The position of its other members towards that determinate superior is a state of subjection or a state of dependence. The mutual relation which subsists between that superior and them may be styled the relation of sovereign and subject, or the relation of sovereignty and subjection."

The most practically important class of political communities, in which it is difficult to say that a sovereign body, in the strictly legal or Austinian sense of the term, exists, is that which is marked by the possession of what are most conveniently called rigid constitutions. By a rigid constitution is meant one which is written, and which marks out in clearly defined terms the powers of the different organs of government, powers which cannot be altered by any legislative body. Such are the constitutions of France and the United States of America. They stand in sharp contrast with the British constitution, which is conveniently said to be of the flexible type; that is to say, it is not strictly set out in any document, but can be altered at will by the Legislature. In England the constitution can be amended or altered to any extent by an ordinary Act of Parliament; a federal constitution for the British Empire could, for instance, be enacted in this way. But in France or the United States the constitution cannot be altered a hair's breadth by ordinary proceedings in the Legislature. This could only be done in some cumbrous or round-about fashion laid down by the constitution itself. A curious result of this is that, in England, alterations in the constitution, amounting in fact to revolutions, have worked their way, almost unobserved, with slow and silent insinuations. Such a real revolution is the system of cabinet government; and yet no one can assign any date for its creation. In France, on the other hand, a change of a much less sweeping kind plunges the whole nation into the throes of a civil disturbance. And, somewhat unfairly, France has won the reputation of a most revolutionary country. Whatever its defects, a flexible constitution has at least the merits of rendering change possible without revolution. Now, in the British constitution there is no difficulty at all in saying where sovereignty lies. That it lies in Parliament, which consists of the Crown and the House of Lords and the House of Commons, may be affirmed without hesitation. Austin, indeed, for want of seeing the distinction between legal and political sovereignty, went out of his way to say that in England sovereignty lies in the Crown, the House of Lords, and the House of Commons, or electors. He imagined that members of the House of Commons represented the electors merely as delegates, and that the electors were actually, through the medium of their representatives, a part of Parliament. There is a partial truth in this, for there is a growing tendency for members of the House of Commons to be returned with cut-and-dried instructions from their constituencies. But it is very far from being the whole truth. Parliament is in fact, as well as in theory, so far sovereign that it can, if it wishes, override the wishes of the people. The manner in which the Septennial Act was passed is enough to put the true sovereignty of Parliament beyond all reasonable doubt. The Parliament that passed that Act was elected for three years only, but it prolonged its own life for seven years, and in all probability prolonged it in the teeth of a hostile people, who would never have elected a Parliament with a mandate to pass such an Act. There can be no doubt, then, where sovereignty lies in the British constitution. And it may fairly be said of any other flexible con-stitution, that it would be easy to put one's finger on the sovereign body with an unerring certainty. But when we come to examine rigid constitutions, it is not always apparent which is the sovereign body and where it lies. In the case of France, and other similar constitutions of a non-composite character, not much difficulty is presented. In France we have already seen that the Legislature is not sovereign, because its powers are limited by the constitution. But behind the Legislature slumbers a body invested with powers which the Legislature does not possess. This is the sovereign body. In France this body is the National Assembly, which consists of the Chamber of Deputies and the Senate sitting together. But in federal constitutions, like that of the United States of America or Switzerland, the question becomes much more difficult. In America the federal and the state Legislatures are certainly not sovereign; neither is the Supreme Court or the President. Some eminent American lawyers are of opinion that there is no legally sovereign body in the United States, and Professor Dicey says that he sees no absurdity in such a supposition. If there is a sovereign body in the United States it must be the body invested by the constitution, with the power of altering that constitution. Article V. of the United States constitution provides that Congress, whenever two-thirds of both Houses shall deem it necessary, shall propose amendments to the constitution, or, on the application of the Legislatures of two-thirds of the several states, shall call a convention for proposing amendments, which in either case shall be valid to all intents and purposes as part of the constitution when ratified by the Legislatures of three-fourths of the several states or by conventions in three-fourths thereof, as the one or the other mode of ratification may be proposed by the Congress. And then follows a proviso, making it illegal to amend certain portions of Article I. prior to the year 1808. So that up to the year 1808, at least, there was no absolutely sovereign body in the United States. Moreover, there is a further proviso that " no state, without its consent, shall be deprived of its equal suffrage in the Senate." So that here there is a check upon the action of the majority of three-fourths of the states necessary to carry an amendment, which to this extent derogates from their sovereign powers, if their powers can be called sovereign. So that whether there is even now a sovereign body in the United States may well be doubted; but if there is a sovereign body, it must be a body consisting of a majority of three-fourths of the several States at any time belonging to the union.

There are two remarkable consequences that flow from sovereignty which should be particularly noted in connection with federal constitutions. One such consequence is that, whereas a sovereign body may delegate its powers of legislation, a non-sovereign body may not. The maxim, " Delegata potestas non delegatur," is here applicable. The powers of the British Parliament differ greatly from those of the American Congress or an American State Legislature. The British Parliament may, in virtue of its inherent original authority, delegate powers to anybody it pleases. It might confer direct legislative powers upon the whole body of the electors, if it chose; as a fact, it has conferred such powers upon the Crown in Council. The American Congress, or an American State Legislature, has no such power as this. They have, indeed, claimed such power, but the American Courts have decided against them, and they have been compelled to give up such pretensions. Another consequence is that no sovereign body can limit its own powers. It is of the essence of sovereignty that there should be unlimited powers. If powers are limited, then *ipso facto* sovereignty vanishes. Any attempt of a sovereign body to limit its own powers must ultimately fail. Some of the Greek republics attempted to render some laws immutable by enacting the death penalty for any one who proposed to repeal them. Just as though it was not obviously easy to first of all propose the repeal of the law enacting the death penalty. The British Parliament is not likely to be suspected of any wish to limit its own powers. Like all other legislatures, it has an insatiable appetite for authority. Yet an instance of such a wish of the British Parliament has been pointed out by Professor Bryce. In the Act of Union with Ireland it was provided that the maintenance of the Protestant Episcopal Church as an Established Church in Ireland should be "deemed an essential and fundamental part of the Union." In 1869 that proviso was cast to the winds; the Protestant Episcopal Church was disestablished without any qualms of conscience whatever.

These two attributes of sovereignty, the one positive, the other negative, should be very fully weighed by those who advocate imperial federation, or would throw our constitution into the melting-pot, and recast it as a brand-new federation of the four several parts of the United Kingdom. For it seems to follow that, if the British Parliament were to create a federation, being a sovereign body, it could not only delegate its powers to any extent, which the other provincial Parliaments could not, but also (which is far more important), as the possessor of unlimited powers, which it could not cut down, it could at any time withdraw from or break up the federal union. It would occupy a superior position to the legislative bodies of the other members of the union. Such a position would contain within itself the seeds of conflict. It would, however, be quite possible for the British people to first annihilate their Parliament, and then to proceed to form a federation, in which a newly created Parliament at Westminster would only have equal powers with those of the other provincial legislatures.

There is one event which might happen to any constitution, whether flexible or rigid, and which, if it did happen, would make it difficult to say that any sovereign body existed. This is the event of civil war or revolution, when the sovereign power is for the time being thrown into abeyance. When, for instance, Charles I. was engaged in fighting his Parliament, it would be impossible to say that any truly sovereign body then existed. The sovereign power is, in fact, the subject of contention, and anarchy for the instant prevails. And Sir James Stephen is of opinion that even where there is no civil war, there may be what he calls dormant anarchy, as was the case in the United States before the war of secession. It was like the sultriness of the air before the bursting of the storm.

Another case of difficulty in saying whether sove-

reignty exists has been suggested by Sir H. S. Maine.
He refers to the cases of oriental communities, both
ancient and modern. The oriental community of
to-day bears a strong likeness to what we know of
similar communities of antiquity. So conservative are
the peoples of the East, and so bound are they in the
swaddling clothes of custom, that many things of a vast
antiquity are to this day preserved amongst them. In
looking to-day on a Hindoo village community, we see
much preserved in a full vitality which existed when
Homer sang, and when the seven hills of Rome were
still untenanted. It is with regard to these oriental
communities, where custom is all-powerful and all-per-
vading, that Sir H. S. Maine has raised difficulties and
opened up a field of inquiry of very great interest; he
has pointed out that sovereignty, as defined by Austin,
is in many ways inapplicable to oriental communities.
It is an essential part of the Austinian conception of
a sovereign body that it should be the source of
positive law, or, in other words, that it should legislate.
Now, it has been shown by Sir H. S. Maine that in
oriental empires there is no sovereign body in this
sense of the term. In these empires anything in the
nature of law has no connection with the sovereign
body. The case of Runjeet Singh, the conqueror and
ruler of the Sikhs, in the Punjaub, is an admirable
instance. How can he be said to have been sovereign
in the Austinian sense of the term? He doubtless
issued particular commands in abundance, and was
implicitly obeyed. He raised taxes and levied armies
and punished the disobedient with death. But he

never legislated. The saying, "Rex les loquens, lex rex loquens," was the reverse of applicable to him. The case of the vassalage of the Jews to Persia is another instance. The Jews continued to live under their own laws, but the Great King never legislated for them. He raised taxes and levied troops, and having done this, he was content to leave them to live pretty much as they pleased. Another instance, which is not oriental, is that of the Athenian republic, which raised taxes from its dependencies, but never legislated for them. In such communities as these, the rules, whether they be called customs or laws, under which men live their lives from day to day, did not have their source in the sovereign body, nor did they receive any sanction from it. They had their source in religion and custom, and their sanction in public opinion and an awe-inspiring superstition. Such works as the Koran and the Institutes of Menu are really the statute-books of the East. But anything in the nature of legislation, or law sanctioned by the sovereign body, there is not. In such matters the sovereign is generally passive. Absolute legislative inactivity is the mark or note of oriental sovereignty. The law of the Medes and Persians that altereth not is the prevailing type of law in the East.

The maxim that "what the sovereign permits, he commands" has been invoked for the purpose of showing that such oriental sovereign bodies as we have described do really legislate. There is, however, a vast difference between the customary law of England, for instance, and that of the East. In England the sovereign body would, if it thought fit, change, and as a matter of fact often does change, the existing common law by statutory enactment. The Married Women's Property Acts, for instance, revolutionized the common law that regulated the relations of husband and wife. But in the East the sovereign body would not dream of doing any such thing. To meddle with the customary law would be deemed a species of impiety. So that, whilst the English sovereign body clearly regards the customary law as coming within the range of its interference, the oriental sovereign body just as clearly regards it as being outside that range. Professor Holland has endeavoured, in his Jurisprudence, to meet the difficulty by suggesting that only those customs are laws which would in case of necessity be enforced by the sovereign body, whereas those which might be habitually disobeyed with impunity are not really laws at all. There is some truth in this, but it presents a difficulty, inasmuch as it would be impossible to say whether a particular custom was a law or not, until it was put to the practical test of being habitually disobeyed with impunity. However that may be, it still remains the fact that the sovereign bodies of the East are non-legislative bodies, while, on the other hand, in the West legislation has become to be considered the pre-eminent mark of sovereignty. Legislation is part of its connotation. The two ideas are inseparable. Something will be said of the United States later on, but it may here be noted that the United States in one way resembles an oriental empire. In the latter the sovereign body does not legislate; in the former the sovereign body (if it exists) does not legislate either, but delegates its legislative powers to subordinate bodies. Moreover, in both cases, as we have seen, it is doubtful whether there really exists any truly sovereign body, though the grounds of doubt are in each case different.

How it came about that legislative activity became to be the most important mark of sovereignty is a curious and interesting inquiry. Sir H. S. Maine thinks that the process began with the Roman Empire, which was the first great empire to legislate. With the fall of the empire the Western World once more relapsed into the old state of things, which was immutable and monotonous. It was only by slow degrees and faltering steps that legislation grew into an important part of sovereignty. It is the most notable thing in the history of its development. The British Parliament is an instance in point. It seems to have been summoned by the kings in early times to impose taxes in order to raise money to supply the king's wants and provide for carrying on war. But legislation (other than money Bills) was very scanty. Even the Great Charter was deemed to be no enactment of new laws, but only a declaration or reassertion of old laws that had fallen into disuse. Gradually legislation became more abundant, but it was not until the time of Bentham that it received any great impetus. Bentham had, however, very decided notions of the purposes for which Government exists. In his opinion the protection of life and property, and the carrying on of the ordinary administrative business of the

nation, was very far from being the whole function of
Government. That function was, he thought, the
promotion of the greatest happiness of the greatest
number. The present century has been remarkable
for the legislative activity of our Parliament, and it is
not too much to say that it is largely due to his
influence. Probably no writer ever lived whose pen
has so altered the course of history.

Since legislation has been so elevated as to have
become almost the chief function of Government and
the most important mark of sovereignty, it is an
interesting inquiry in what manner modern states
have made provision for the exercise of the legislative
function, and what are the relations borne by the
executive to the legislature. We have seen that in
oriental empires legislation is commonly thrown into
the background. The executive functions are everything, and the legislative nothing. Runjeet Singh
and his advisers (if he had any) formed an admirable
executive within the comparatively narrow sphere of
action to which they confined their energies. He formed
a most efficient Chancellor of the Exchequer, War Sec-
retary, and Commander-in-Chief. He was as successful
in raising funds as he was in levying troops. But here
his functions ended; while as to legislation, he never
attempted it. A sovereign body, therefore, on its
executive side, resembles an oriental sovereignty;
whilst, on its legislative side, it is of the nature of
sovereignty in its modern and European sense. The
executive and the legislature are, putting the judiciary
aside, the two great elements of sovereignty—the

former coming down from a hoar antiquity, and still lingering on in the East in a masterful exclusiveness; the latter of more modern origin, but growing from strength to strength, and, by its encroachments on the former, winning for itself an equal, if not the first, place in the state. It is remarkable, indeed, how constantly the legislature tends to encroach on the executive. It seems to have been thought by political philosophers that the three great elements of sovereignty, the legislature, the executive and the judicial, or at least the two former, should be kept entirely distinct and independent of one another. Aristotle led the way. "All states have three elements, and the good lawgiver has to regard what is expedient for each state. When they are well ordered, the state is well ordered, and as they differ from one another, constitutions differ. What is the element, first, which deliberates about public affairs; secondly, which is concerned with the magistrates, and determines what they should be, over whom they should exercise authority, and what should be the mode of electing them; and, thirdly, which has judicial power?" Locke says "that the legislative and executive powers are in distinct hands in all moderated monarchies and well-framed governments." Montesquieu was the first to make the theory a generally accepted one amongst political thinkers, and Blackstone follows him in laying down that "whenever the power of making and that of enforcing laws are united together, there can be no public liberty. Where the legislative and executive authority are in distinct hands, the former will take care not to

C

trust the latter with so large a power as may tend to the subversion of its own independence, and therewith of the liberty of the subject." This distribution of powers into separate hands was regarded by the architects of the American constitution as a political maxim, and that constitution was avowedly founded upon it. Yet the practice by no means squares with the theory. The twin organs of Government are in reality too interdependent to be kept apart, and where the executive has, in the opinion of the legislature, arrogated too much to itself, the latter has generally, at least in the Western world, wrestled with it for supremacy and has prevailed. It has, indeed, done more than prevail; it has grappled with its adversary, and has subdued it utterly to its will. The gradual encroachment of the legislature on the executive can be noticed in very early times. In the old Greek Republics, the assembly of the citizens not only passed laws, but performed executive acts, such as making peace or declaring war, with equal facility. They gave executive orders, or ψήφισματα, with the same ease as they passed laws, or νόμοι. The Roman Comitia constantly did the same thing. In England the conflict between the executive and the legislature forms a great part of the history of the country. The Crown and its ministers formed the executive, and originally they formed an executive of a very independent character. But the legislature wrestled with it and gradually encroached on its powers, and finally succeeded in bending them to its will. As a result we now find that the Cabinet ministers, who form the real executive (the Crown being reduced to a merely nominal possession of power), not only form part of the legislature, but the most important part of it. It is not only considered essential that a Cabinet minister should sit in Parliament, but the Cabinet is regarded as a sort of committee of a party majority for framing legislative proposals. It is now almost the sole source of law-making. So long ago as 1848, Lord John Russell, in a speech in the House of Commons, remarked upon the change that had taken place. He said, "There have been, in the course of the last thirty years, very great changes in the mode of conducting the business of the House. When I first entered Parliament, it was not usual for Government to undertake generally all subjects of legislation; . . . since the passing of the Reform Bill, it has been thought convenient, on every subject on which an alteration in the law is required, that the Government should undertake the responsibility of proposing it to Parliament." Cabinets are judged much more by their success or failure in carrying through legislation than by their executive acts. The present Cabinet gained more discredit by failing to carry through the Irish Land Bill and the Tithes Bill than it gained *éclat* by successfully negotiating treaties about Africa with Germany and France. As Professor Bryce says, "They are not merely executive agents, but also legislative leaders." And, as Sir H. S. Maine says, the British constitution is paradoxical. "While the House of Commons has assumed the supervision of the whole executive government, it has turned over to the executive the

most important of the business of legislation." The
legislature now executes, while the executive legislates.
To such an extent are the legislature and executive
now interwoven. It is true, indeed, that in foreign
affairs the executive still retains a good idea of
independence and freedom from legislative control,
because promptitude and secrecy are here indispensable,
though even here the approval of Parliament must be
virtually obtained for such important matters as
declaring war or concluding treaties. In all other
departments legislative control is complete. A vast
change indeed from the time when the executive was
the dominant power. As might have been expected,
it proved restive under the attempts of the legislature
to curb it. As the saying is, there was no love lost
between them, and the executive minced no words in
denouncing its enemy. Strafford described the House
of Commons as a "cunning and malicious hydra;"
and Charles I. characteristically remarked that "Parliaments are of the nature of cats that ever grow
curst with age; so that if he will have good of them,
put them off handsomely when they come to any age;
for young ones are ever the most tractable." But the
executive finally succumbed, and, instead of quarrelling
with the legislature, it has become, not only part and
parcel of it, but the most important part of it. They
are equal yoke-fellows under the orders of the great
British public that lies behind them. The British
sovereign body has in short lost, in a large degree,
what may be called its purely ancient and oriental
features, or rather it has assumed those legislative

features which are the mark of modern and Western sovereignty. It is not that it has lost its executive powers, for they are still almost as vigorously exercised as ever. But such is its activity as a law-maker, that its work as an administrator, which is carried on unceasingly from day to day and hour to hour, is, comparatively speaking, allowed to drop out of notice. The details of administration are, for the most part, too commonplace to attract attention.

What has been said of British sovereignty may be said also of all British self-governing colonies, and, without much qualification, of all Western European countries. When we come to consider the case of the United States of America, we might reasonably suppose that, in going westward, we should find the same type of government prevailing, only in more marked degree. Yet, on examination, a very great difference is found to exist between the American and British types of government. It is commonly supposed that the American government is like the British, a President being substituted for a monarch, and that it is far more like than the French government. This is the exact opposite of the truth, for the French government is infinitely more like than the American. The difference between the British and American governments consists not merely in the fact that the United States are a confederation, though this is of capital importance. There is a radical difference in the constitution of the federal or central government. We have seen that in the British constitution the executive and the legislature are closely united. In the American constitution an exactly opposite state of things prevails, of which, curiously enough, we may find an example nearer home, in the tiny dependency of the Isle of Man. There the student of politics may study in miniature the American constitution, stripped, of course, of its federal attributes. In America the executive and the legislature are distinct and independent. They were made so by the architects of the American constitution partly on theoretical and partly on historical grounds, which it would be out of place to discuss here. It must be enough to mark the fact. The executive in America has no place in Congress, and has no legislative authority. The relations of the executive to the legislature are in America the exact antithesis of those relations in England. The difference may be shortly summed up by saying that the British government is a parliamentary government, and the American a non-parliamentary one. In the first case the legislature both legislates and governs; in the second case, the legislature legislates, but does not govern. We have seen that in America Congress, which is the legislative body, is not sovereign, for its powers are limited by the constitution. Neither is the President, in whom the executive authority is centred, sovereign, for his powers are limited in a like manner. Both Congress and the President possess, not inherent, but delegated power. The sovereign body in America, if it exists, usually slumbers. But if, as we may for all practical purposes, we consider the executive and the legislature as forming two co-ordinate branches of a sovereign body, it will be seen that, whilst in England

the legislature has become the supreme part of
sovereignty, in America the legislature is not supreme,
but merely co-ordinate. In England the union of the
executive and the legislature is now so complete, that
both work together harmoniously. In America, on the
contrary, there is disunion, and sometimes conflict.
The executive and the legislature are like a pair of
ill-matched horses, that cause the coach of government to creak and sway. Congress can thwart the
President, but the President can revenge himself by
thwarting Congress. But here also, according to the
general rule before noticed, the legislature tends to
encroach on the executive. It fought with President
Andrew Johnson and defeated him. It has devised a
method of thwarting the President by tacking on to
money Bills provisions that have nothing to do with
the financial part of them. In much the same way
the French Chambers have discovered a method of
overcoming their President by the refusal of any
member to take office under any President they dislike.
President Grévy was compelled to leave the Elysée,
although by law he was fully entitled to remain. But
in spite of the tendency of the legislature to encroach,
the American executive has much greater powers,
which it can exercise independently, than the British
executive has. The American President is, during
his term of office, a much more powerful person than
the British monarch or the French President. He
governs as well as reigns. The executive really holds
a much more important place in the American than in
the British constitution. Not that the British execu-

tive is weak, but that its real power is concealed and swallowed up in the legislature. But in America there is, in a sense, a reversion to the old or oriental type of sovereignty, of which the chief characteristic is the existence of an Executive enjoying absolutely uncontrolled authority. That there is plenty of legislation in America no one can doubt. There is, indeed, more than is altogether agreeable to the average American citizen, who is apt to grow disgusted with the "logrolling" and "lobbying" that haunts the legislative chambers. This is more true of the State legislatures than it is of Washington. The Americans distrust their law-makers; they agree with Charles the First, and take care that their Parliaments do not become "curst with age" by giving them a short lease of life, and they try to render them powerless by dividing them into two chambers that are likely to disagree. M. Thiers used to say that a republic was best for France, because it divided Frenchmen least. Conversely, the Americans think that two chambers are best for them, because it divides their legislators most. They even look to the executive to protect them from the legislature, and admire a President who makes a bold use of the veto. President Cleveland was liked none the worse for vetoing a number of Bills providing pensions for combatants in the War of Secession. But in spite of all this energy expended in legislation or attempted legislation, the fact still remains that in America there stands out a clearly cut and independent executive, which is in type more oriental than European.

We have spoken of the distrust displayed in America for legislative bodies. This distrust is not so widely felt in England, but signs of it are not wanting. The House of Commons certainly commands less respect than it did. In France, Mr. Hamerton, who is an excellent judge, says that the Senate and Chamber of Deputies command no respect whatever. It is, indeed, quite within the bounds of possibility that means will be devised of putting the activity of legislators under restraint, and that a more purely executive form of sovereignty will be reverted to. The pendulum of sovereignty has swung from a pure executive without legislation to the other extreme of an executive trammelled on all sides with legislation. There are now signs that the pendulum has begun to swing the other way. There is good reason for believing that democracies are not so prone to change as is generally believed. Sir H. S. Maine has eloquently shown that change is not only not desired, but is positively abhorred by a great part of the human race. The experience derived from the use of the Referendum in Switzerland is evidence of the same thing. The Swiss have by their popular vote rejected a surprising number of the measures which they have been asked to pass by the federal chambers. It is an undeniable and unfortunate fact that many Bills are introduced for purely party purposes. Promises are made by candidates on the hustings which have to be redeemed in Parliament. Bills are so much bait to catch popular votes. Moreover, popular leaders may be perfectly sincere and yet hold views far in advance of the mass of society. Some of the most prominent of our Australasian public men hold views on land and other questions far in advance of the people at large. In America, as we have said, the State legislatures make experiments that bring on themselves ridicule, if not odium. Laws are not always there what Demosthenes said they were—the gifts of the gods, and the discovery of sages. The law-makers at Albany, in the State of New York, who were responsible for Kremmler's execution by electricity, simply outraged humanity. The feeling is beginning to grow both in Europe and America that the more Bills a legislature kills, the better. A small class of thinkers are beginning to see that legislation is by no means an unmixed blessing. Mr. Herbert Spencer, in his " Man *versus* the State," quotes from a paper read by Mr. Janson before the Statistical Society in 1873. Mr. Janson states that of the Public Acts passed from the Statute of Merton (20 Henry III.) to the end of 1872, no less than four-fifths had been repealed; and that in the short space of three years, 1870–73, no less than 3532 Public Acts had been repealed wholly or in part or amended, and 2759 had been wholly repealed. Mr. Spencer further states that he has found by his own investigation (in the year 1884) that during the three previous sessions there had been repealed 650 Acts of the present reign, besides many of preceding reigns. After making due allowance for repeals due to laws becoming obsolete, or being inoperative, or to consolidation, he concludes that a large residuum must have been repealed because they were found to be injurious. And he goes on to say, and rightly say, "That bad legislation means injury to men's lives." "Judge," he says, "what must be the total amount of mental distress, physical pain, and raised mortality, which these thousands of repealed Acts of Parliament represent!" On the ground of these considerations, it is not unreasonable to suppose that some means will be sooner or later found for checking legislatures, and for making sovereignty a more purely executive organ. The Americans have made a nearer approach to this than the British have, and some of their best authorities are of opinion that some means will have to be devised by us, and that soon, for rendering it less easy to make changes that affect our constitution. Our practice seems to them dangerously lax.

The question of legal and political sovereignty has already been mentioned. The distinction between the two is so important that it deserves a very full consideration. It has already been said that the British Parliament is sovereign, because it enjoys unlimited powers. But every one knows that there is a great deal which Parliament dare not do, which it might theoretically do. It might declare murder legal, if it dared. It is apparent, then, that though it is legally sovereign, it is not politically sovereign. Its omnipotence is restricted by what Austin calls positive morality. There is a political sovereign behind it, and that political sovereign is the people. Rousseau was in a great degree right when he said that the legislator is the servant of the sovereign people. It may not be true of Russia or Siam, but is quite true of England and France. Burke said that "in all forms of government the people is the true legislator." That is too general a statement. It is true of many forms of government, though not of all. It is only another way of asserting the growth of democracy, which is in these days a fact, whether an agreeable one or not. From the time when Plato spoke contemptuously of "the many-headed" until quite recently, popular rule has been utterly scorned. It may be even asserted that democracy is a perfectly modern institution. Mr. Grote, in his monumental work on the "History of Greece," went to much pains to defend the Athenian democracy. Yet, when it is considered that what are now called the lower classes were represented by slaves in Greece, it may well be doubted whether Athens was a democracy at all. It was a republic, no doubt, but a republic is not necessarily a democracy. Democracy is simply the rule of the majority. However that may be (putting ancient history aside), democracy is a modern institution. The mediæval republics of Italy were probably more oligarchical than democratic. Lord Bacon declared that he hated the word "people." Cardinal Granvelle, the ally of Spain in its conflict with popular liberties in the Netherlands, spoke of the people as "a vile and mischievous animal." Even Pope could write of the aristocracy of his time—

> "So much they scorn the crowd, that if the throng
> By chance go right, they purposely go wrong."

But at the present time, in all civilized communities, except Russia and the East, δημὸς is king. It is clear, therefore, that there have now arisen two independent sovereignties in the state—the legal sovereign and the political sovereign. It becomes, therefore, an important question how far these two sovereignties can be made to work in harmony. If no means can be found to secure this harmonious working, there will be civil conflict and strife. There can be no middle course, for the conduct of one can by no means be a matter of indifference to the other. This end is obtained in different ways in different forms of government; and there are few things more interesting in politics than an examination of what these different ways are. In the British Islands, this end is to some extent reached by the firm hold which the legislature has taken of the executive. It is true that the monarch, who centres in himself the executive, holds an hereditary office. But he is only a formal head, who acts upon the advice of his Prime Minister, who is the real head. Now, as the Prime Minister is dependent upon a popularly elected House of Commons, the people obtain, in roundabout fashion, a control over the acts of the hereditary monarch. The same thing may be truly said of all constitutional monarchies, and it is also true of such a President as the French President, who acts upon the advice of the French Prime Minister. In the United States, the President is elected directly by an electoral college and ultimately by the people. And though the popular will has been largely ignored under the exigencies of the electoral machines, still the people have a strong hold over the President. A President who defies the popular

will bids good-bye to all chances of re-election. But
this is not all. In England the harmonious co-
operation of the legal and political sovereignties is in
a great degree secured by what are known as "constitutional conventions." Their nature is admirably
explained by Professor Dicey in his "Law of the
Constitution." "Their object is," he says, "to give
effect to the will of the political sovereign; they are
precepts for determining the mode and spirit in which
the prerogative is to be exercised." The word prerogative is one of which it is not easy to grasp the
full meaning. It has a history which is suggestive of
despotism, and savours of monarchical interference.
The popular idea of it was expressed by Lord John
Russell, when he said that if the sword of prerogative was drawn, it was time to be prepared with
the shield and buckler of popular privileges. The
prerogative of the Crown is still much greater than is
commonly supposed. Mr. Bagehot wrote of the powers
of the Queen as follows: " Not to mention other things,
she could disband the army (by law she cannot engage
more than a certain number of men, but she is not
obliged to engage any men); she could dismiss all the
officers, from the general commanding-in-chief down-
wards; she could dismiss all the sailors too; she
could sell off all our ships of war, and all our naval
stores; she could make peace by the sacrifice of
Cornwall, and begin a new war for the conquest of
Brittany. She could make every citizen in the United
Kingdom, male or female, a peer; she could make
every parish in the United Kingdom a university; she

could dismiss most of the civil servants; she could pardon all offenders." It is clear, then, that the prerogative is very large; but in whatever way it was once used, it is now used in such a manner as to ensure the supremacy of the true political sovereign, or the people. It is, in the words of Professor Dicey, "nothing else than the residue of discretionary or arbitrary authority, which at any given time is legally left in the hands of the Crown," and is now always used in the manner indicated. It was long before the Crown acquiesced in this view of the exercise of the prerogative, and it was sometimes supported by its advisers. Lord Shelburne, for instance, said that "he would never consent that the King of England should be a king of the Mahrattas; for among the Mahrattas the custom is, it seems, for a certain number of great lords to elect a peishwah, who is thus the creature of the aristocracy, and is vested with the plenitude of power, while their king is, in fact, nothing more than a royal pageant." George the Third strongly objected to being nothing more than a royal pageant, and made strenuous endeavours to govern as well as reign. But the House of Commons put a check upon kingly pretensions by affirming, in 1780, Mr. Dunning's resolution, "that the influence of the Crown has increased, is increasing, and ought to be diminished." Perhaps the best example of the way in which the Crown uses its prerogative to ensure harmony between the legal and political sovereigns is that involved in the dissolution of Parliament. In 1784 George the Third dismissed a ministry which had the confidence of the House of

Commons, because he thought that the wishes of the legislature diverged from those of the nation. He was, as the result showed, right in his belief. In 1834 William the Fourth dismissed a ministry on the same grounds, though events showed that his action was not justified by the facts. The dissolution of Parliament in 1841, though in less striking degree than the examples already given, is a good example of the use of the prerogative. That Parliament was elected to support the interests of Protection, but it committed itself to the policy of Free Trade. It was chosen to substitute Sir R. Peel for Lord John Russell, but it restored Lord John Russell to the position from which Sir Robert Peel had driven him. It therefore became very apparent that the legislature and the electors might well be at variance, and a dissolution was justly considered necessary. The demand for triennial Parliaments is invariably made, it should be observed, by the party in opposition, on the ground that Parliament has ceased to represent the popular feeling. A very strong use of the prerogative was made in 1871, when Mr. Gladstone failed to get through the Lords a Bill for the abolition of purchase in the army, which had been passed by the Commons. The Queen, on his advice, thereupon abolished the system in virtue of her prerogative. The act was strongly objected to at the time by the late Mr. Fawcett and others, but there can be little doubt it tended to harmonize the legal and political sovereigns. It is somewhat singular that in the last session of Parliament Mr. Gladstone objected that it was an encroachment upon the prerogative to introduce a Bill for the cession of Heligoland, when such a Bill might have been dispensed with. But this really was not the case, as Mr. Gladstone's own action in 1871 shows. In either case the political sovereignty of the people is assured. If the House of Commons is in harmony with the electors, there can be no objection to procedure by Bill; if they are not in harmony, or if the Lords are obstructive, the prerogative can override them both, and the people will prevail.

The most direct and the simplest way of ensuring the supremacy of the political sovereign is to be found in Switzerland. The method in operation there is one of the political curiosities of the world. Nowhere else in the world can it be found in a fully developed state. This is a device by which, when the circumstances provided by the constitution demand it, Bills before the Federal Legislature (or the Canton Legislature, as the case may be) are referred to direct popular vote. In addition to this, in some of the cantons the people are enabled to introduce legislation by means of the "Initiative." But the Referendum is by far the most important of the two. It is obvious that in this way the people of Switzerland get a most complete control over their legislature. Strictly speaking, no doubt, the legislature is not legally sovereign, for, as the Swiss constitution is rigid, it has strictly limited powers. But, for all practical purposes, we may consider it legally sovereign, and if we do so, it will be at once seen, by means of the Referendum, that the political sovereign of Switzerland is brought into harmonious relations with the

D

legal sovereign. The latter can by no means override the will of the former; on the contrary, if a conflict arises, the latter must automatically, so to speak, give way.

Whether the Referendum should be introduced into the British constitution or not, is a question that has given rise to considerable discussion, and much difference of opinion. Professor Bryce thinks that its introduction would be advantageous. It would transfer the power of dissent or the royal prerogative of vetoing legislation from the Crown to the people. This would be beneficial, inasmuch as it would withdraw legislation from the absolute control of party political feeling, make members of Parliament more independent, and lessen the influence of cliques and sections. Professor Bryce is, however, fully alive to its difficulties. He sees that it would be difficult of application in a country as large and as populous as the United Kingdom. Moreover, it would be difficult to define the particular class of Bills to which it should be applied. Supposing it were to be confined to Bills proposing constitutional changes only, it would sometimes be difficult to say whether certain changes were strictly constitutional or not. Then, again, there are certain measures, which are of far greater importance than some constitutional changes, which, upon this supposition, would not be submitted to the Referendum. A difficulty, also, would arise over the means of testing separately English, Scotch, and Irish opinion. Lastly, useful measures, which did not happen to excite general interest, would run great risk of being rejected. This is shown to have actually happened in Switzerland. The amount of political apathy in the country is larger than is commonly supposed. The number of abstainers from voting can only be accounted for in this way. Madame de Stael used to say, " Parler politique, pour moi c'est vivre." The ordinary voter is very far from being in a like case. On the contrary, as Conversation Sharpe said, most men like to have their thinking, like their washing, done out. Professor Dicey, too, makes two far-reaching objections to its introduction. He thinks, first, that it would lower the importance of Parliament ; and, secondly, that it would be an appeal from a higher class to a lower class. It is a remarkable thing, too, that Mr. Grote, the champion of democracy, severely condemned the Referendum when it was first introduced into the constitution of Lucerne. Whether Professor Dicey's objections are well founded or not is doubtful. It will be answered differently, according to the estimation in which Parliament is held by different minds. His objections will have no weight with those who despise Parliament, and place the people above their representatives. If, however, the Referendum should at any time be introduced into the British constitution, it would mark the consummation of a tendency that has been long developing. This tendency is the transfer of authority from the Crown to the people. By it the royal prerogative of veto would be transferred to the people. At one time this prerogative of the Crown was a very real power. In the year 1597, Elizabeth is said to have vetoed forty-eight bills out of ninety-three. William III.

vetoed five bills, and in 1757 it was made use of for
the last time by Anne, over a Scotch Militia Bill.
This power. has long ceased to be exercised. It is a
weapon which the Crown has long feared to use. But
by means of the Referendum it would be transferred
to the people, who, having nothing to fear, would use
it with the same freedom that the Crown did. In the
hands of the people, the weapon that lay unsheathed
and rusty in the royal armoury would be bright and
burnished. This at least would be a change for the
better.

> "How dull it is to pause, to make an end,
> To rust unburnished, not to shine in use!"

Isocrates long ago expressed an opinion that the men
of wealth and leisure should be the servants of the
people, and that the people should, in his own emphatic
words, be a tyrant. The introduction of the Referendum would still leave the opinion of Isocrates in the
realm of ideals, and a counsel of perfection. It would,
however, make doubly true the saying that democracy
is monarchy inverted. It would ensure, also, the con-
tinuance of harmony between the legal and political
sovereigns—a harmony that will alone prevent democracy from falling into anarchy, and which, if unattained
and unattainable, would relegate the rule of the people
to the limbo of impracticable ideals.

II.

FEDERAL GOVERNMENT.

We live in an age of union. Individuals now unite and agree to sink their differences for all kinds of purposes, whether for private gain or for propagating views, or attaining ends, in morals, politics, religion, science, or art. It is a time of associations, unions, and leagues. And so it is with states. They are in this respect the man writ large. For one of the most remarkable phenomena in politics of the last hundred years is the impetus that has been given to the development of federal institutions. There are to-day contemporaneously existing no less than ten distinct federal governments. First and foremost is the United States of America, where we have an example of the federal union in the most perfect form yet attained. Then comes Switzerland, of less importance than the United States, but most nearly approaching it in perfection. Again, there is the German Empire, that great factor in European politics, which is a truly federal union, but a cumbrous one, and full of anomalies. Next in importance comes the Dominion of Canada, which, except the West Indian Leeward Islands, is the only example of a country forming a federal union, and at the same time a colony. Then come the Argentine Republic, Mexico, and the states of Colombia and Venezuela. Last in point of time is Brazil, which first dismissed its Emperor, and then proceeded to federate its vast and thinly peopled provinces. It now calls itself the United States of Brazil.

This is a very remarkable list, when we consider that never before the present century did more than two federal unions ever co-exist, and that very rarely, and that even those unions were far from satisfying the true requirements of federation. Nor is this all. Throughout the last hundred years we can mark a growing tendency in countries that have adopted the federal type of government to perfect that federal type, and make it more truly federal than before. In the United States of America, for instance, the Constitution of 1789 was more truly federal than the Confederation, and certainly since the civil war we hear less of state rights, and more of union. It has, indeed, been remarked that the citizens of the United States have become fond of applying the words " nation " and " national " to themselves in a manner formerly unknown. We can mark the same progress in Switzerland. Before 1789 Switzerland formed a very loose system of confederated states. There was then little more than an alliance of Cantons, that received and sent their own embassies. The founders of the American union deliberately rejected it as a model for this very reason. But in 1815 a constitution more truly federal was devised; in 1848 the federal union was more firmly consolidated; and, lastly, in 1874 such changes were made in the constitution, that Switzerland now presents a fairly perfect example of federal government. In Germany we may trace a similar movement. In 1815 the Germanic confederation was formed, but it was only a system of confederated states, or what the Germans call Staatenbund; but after various changes, amongst others the exclusion of Austria in 1866, it became in 1871 a composite state, or, in German language, a Bundestaat.

So far we have dealt with accomplished facts. Tendencies in the direction of federation still remain, some of them at present insignificant, and some fraught with great consequences. We will take the minor ones first. In South Africa attempts have been made to federate the South African colonies and states, so far without success. The nearest approach to it is the Customs Union, which exists between Cape Colony and the Orange Free State. It is said, however, to be part of the policy of Mr. Cecil Rhodes, the present Premier at the Cape, to try to carry out federation. And when it is considered that the feelings of antipathy between the Dutch and English residents are subsiding, that railways are spreading, and that the Transvaal is being rapidly Anglicized, it must be admitted that the dream is not an idle one. It is a long way from South Africa to Central America. But even in backward Central America federation has been in the air, and San Salvador and Guatemala came to blows over this very question quite recently. The federation of the Leeward Islands has already

been named, and it is interesting to observe that these
islands enjoyed a federal union from the time of
William and Mary until the end of last century.
The union then fell to pieces, but was reconstituted
in Mr. Gladstone's first administration. But the noteworthy point here is the spread of federal ideas in the
West Indies. Some sort of union already exists
between Jamaica and Turk's Island, Trinidad and
Tobago, and amongst the Windward Islands, and there
is a growing feeling towards federation. Federation
is regarded by some as the destination of the Balkan
Principalities, but the idea is at present quite without
the range of practical politics.

There remain some manifestations of tendency
towards federation of much greater importance. The
first of these is Australian federation. This has been
in a large measure accomplished. In the year 1886
a Bill passed the Imperial Parliament to permit the
formation of an Australasian Council for the purpose
of forming the Australasian colonies into a federation.
This Council has actually been formed, but so far
New South Wales and New Zealand have failed to
come in. It is authorized to legislate directly with
regard to Australasian interests in the Pacific, Australasian fisheries, services of process in other colonies,
extradition, and the influx of criminals. In other
matters, with regard to which the colonies themselves
can legislate, action by the Council can only be taken
after two colonies have brought the matter before the
Council, and even then, any acts passed by the Council
affect those colonies only by whose legislatures the

matters in question have been referred to it. This Council has met several times, and seems likely to grow in favour and authority. Sir Samuel Griffith, the Premier of Queensland, announced a short time ago, at the opening of his Parliament, that it was intended to divide Queensland into three federal provinces, and he went on to say that he expected that this group of Queensland states would pass under the control of an Australian Federal Parliament. This statement, coming as it did from the Queensland Premier, is a most important one, and clearly shows that Australian federation is sure to come sooner or later. New South Wales at first refused to entertain the idea, but she took part in the Federation Congress held at Melbourne in February, 1890. Sir Henry Parkes, the Premier of New South Wales, is quite enthusiastic over it, and, in advocating it to his Australian fellow-countrymen, he reminded them of the crimson thread of their common kinship. It seems, therefore, almost certain that Australian federation will be accomplished. Mr. Brunton Stephens writes the following significant lines in the Australian National Anthem, which he has lately composed :—

> "Let us united stand,
> One great Australian band,
> Heart to heart, hand in hand."

Poets are sometimes the first to catch the rising spirit of the age, and sing the strains of prophecy. It is, indeed, within measurable distance of consummation. Australasian federation, which would unite not only the Australian colonies and Tasmania, but also New

Zealand and Fiji, is less probable, because the great distance of New Zealand and Fiji from Australia throw difficulties in the way.

Australian federation leads to the consideration of another tendency in the direction of federal union. This is the great idea of Imperial Federation. Of this all that can be said at present is that it is under discussion. It presents enormous difficulties, and if it comes at all, it is almost sure to come as a natural growth out of present circumstances. Lastly, we hear of further aspirations for applying the federal system, as though there were some peculiar virtue or talismanic effect about it, which rendered it a panacea for all political troubles. Some people think they see a simple solution of the Irish question in the application of federation, particularly the Canadian form of it, to Ireland.

Federation, therefore, has clearly become a very practical question for the British people, and it is obviously necessary to clearly understand its nature. For no one can possibly speak with any approach to correctness on Imperial or Irish federation, unless he understands the nature of a federal union and its practical results.

Moreover, quite apart from practical politics, it has a distinct theoretical interest of its own. In the first place, it was until recently, a very rare product of the human mind. We only know of three well-marked federations which existed prior to the foundation of the United States of America. The first belongs to the ancient world, and to the second and third centuries

B.C.—namely, the Achœan League—which is interesting, if for no other reason than that Hamilton, the master architect of the American constitution, longed to know more about it. The second is Swiss, which, taking its origin as the old league of Upper Germany in the thirteenth century, has lasted in various forms to the present day. The third is the United Netherlands, which arose at the end of the sixteenth century and lasted to the end of the eighteenth. In the next place, federal government is the highest and most complicated of all forms of government, and demands for its successful development some of the highest elements of political morality. It is, therefore, very interesting, when considered in the light of the natural history of political institutions. It is the roof and crown of things political, and forms the concluding member of a series. Beginning with the individual man as the first of the series, we may go through the family, the tribe, the state, in all its varying degrees of development, and finally arrive at that union of states which is known as the federal union. In the language of biology, it may be considered as the full development of what was originally a very simple growth. It is the final result of evolution in institutions of government. The complexities of federation are doubtless the reason why it has developed so late in human history, and it is worthy of note that the first example of it we meet with was the creation of the Greeks, a people endowed with a singular genius for politics, both in the abstract and in their practical application.

Again, it is interesting, because in it we are enabled
to watch the wheels of government moving on a large
scale.   We have no need of a microscopic eye to watch
it.   There is something grand and titanic about it,
when it is viewed working on the scale on which it
now works in the United States of America.   It is not
a matter of observing the minutiæ of the parish, the
township, the county, or any municipal institution,
but the more impressive acts of states, sovereign within
their own limits, combining to form a united government.   The observance of federal government is, compared with the observance of merely municipal and
strictly local phenomena, what the observance of the
movements of the heavenly bodies, describing their
illimitable ellipses and parabolas, is to the observance
of the movements of bacilli through the lens of the
microscope.

Both from its practical and theoretical aspect, it is
evident, then, that federal government is well worthy
of study.   And when a thing is made an object of
study, it is no unreasonable demand that a definition
of it should be given.   But definition is at all times
difficult, and no wise man ever ventures to define
unless under some necessity.   It is almost a hopeless
task, not unlike that imposed on the daughters of
Danaus; for it is nearly impossible to fill up the out-
line of a definition that will hold water.   And the man
who defines may consider himself lucky if he meets
with no worse fate than that ancient philosopher, who,
having defined man as a " featherless biped," was presented with a feathered fowl in proof of the worthless-

ness of his assertion. And when an attempt is made to define something intangible and impalpable, the difficulty becomes far greater. It is better, therefore, not to attempt to define federal government, but as accurately as may be, to set forth its most salient characteristics.

It must, in the first place, be kept distinct from other political unions, such as mere alliances of defence and offence, of which the present Triple Alliance is an example on the one hand, and on the other hand such personal unions under the same crown as Norway and Sweden, Belgium and the Congo Free State, and such real unions under one parliament, as the kingdom of Great Britain and Ireland, and even such a union as that of Austria and Hungary, which, to some extent, resembles a federal union.

A federal union has its origin under very peculiar circumstances, and perhaps the best way of arriving at a clear conception of federal government is to examine the causes that give it creation. " Vere scire est per causas scire," says Lord Bacon; and this is certainly true here. The people who desire federal union must be placed in peculiar circumstances; it has been put well and shortly in this way—that they must desire union, but not desire unity. And it will generally be found that this state of affairs arises under extreme external pressure. The people who unite to form a federal union find that they cannot stand alone, and in order to preserve their independence, they are compelled in the direction of union; but though they desire the strength acquired from the putting together

of common resources, they still desire to retain their
independence. The United Netherlands feared Spain.
The revolted colonies of North America feared that
their independence would fall a sacrifice to British
selfishness, and it is expressly laid down in the Articles
of Confederation that the various states united " for
common defence." Switzerland is perhaps the most
remarkable example of all. The Helvetic Republic
is a most notable union of dissimilar elements. One
may well ask in amazement what in common has the
French-speaking citizen of Geneva with the German-
speaking citizen of Zurich and the Italian-speaking
citizen of Lugano? One may well wonder how it is
that the Ultramontane of Lucerne and the Calvinist
of Zurich ever came to unite at all. We shall see
hereafter that, as a matter of fact, the union was only
accomplished with difficulty. Then, again, the very
geography of the country seems to forbid union.
Torn up and divided by giant mountains, Switzerland
seems the predestined of nature for separation, and
not union. The cause is not far to seek. The Swiss,
beyond all others, love freedom and local autonomy.
They are surrounded by great and powerful neighbours, who even now might proceed to its partition
but for the treaty made at the Congress of Vienna in
1815, which guarantees perpetual neutrality to Swiss
territory. It has been pointed out by a writer in the
Revue des Deux Mondes that Switzerland is hemmed
almost on all sides by the members of the Triple
Alliance, who would not, in case of need, be over-
scrupulous in respecting this neutrality. Union is

life to the Swiss, and the very charter of their existence, and this they have fully recognized. The Union
first of all consisted only of eight Cantons, but it has
gone on increasing, and now numbers twenty-two, and,
as we have seen, has become more and more consolidated.
The same may be said of the German Empire; for,
though it was in 1871, at the conclusion of a great war,
that the present German Constitution was formed, yet it
was the trial of the war that made the separate States
see how important union was, and made the possible
results of disunion stand out in full relief in all their
glaring hideousness. The Dominion of Canada has a
somewhat different origin. It cannot be said that the
federal union of Canada was formed under conditions
of great external pressure. It was, however, seen that
a federal union might prove a solution for the difficult
problem of governing the various Canadian provinces,
and it must not be forgotten that Canada has for a
neighbour the Colossus of the United States, taking
in at a stride a large portion of a continent from ocean
to ocean, and that the pressure of the United States
on the separate and disunited provinces of Canada
might prove irresistible. Indeed, there can be no
doubt that the mere presence of the United States
did much to create the Canadian union of 1867.
Canada seems naturally as ill-adapted for union as
Switzerland. It contains two races of different tongues
and different creeds that are fiercely opposed. These
are the French and British. The census of 1881
showed that Canada contained a population of 1,300,000
French, of whom 1,000,000 lived in the single province

of Quebec. The French Roman Catholics of Quebec
might well feel ill disposed to union with the Protestant British of the other provinces. At that time,
too, when there were no railways, the commercial
interests of the different provinces were opposed. Such
trade as there was lay, not between the provinces themselves, but with the United States. The trade of
Quebec was with the New England States, and that
of Ontario and Manitoba with the Western States. It
became evident, therefore, that a disunited Canada
was drifting towards absorption in the United States,
and the only safeguard lay in the creation of a federal
tie. And, strange though it may appear, the French
colonists were even more eager than the British to
avoid absorption by the United States. For the
French very well knew that their racial idiosyncrasies
would receive scant attention if they were once
swamped and swallowed up amongst the vast population of their American neighbours. As it is, they
are treated tenderly in the Dominion. French, for
instance, can be spoken in the Dominion Parliament,
but it may safely be asserted that the American Congress would never tolerate that. It should not be
forgotten, however, with regard to Canadian federation,
that it is not universally deemed to be a success.
Professor Goldwin Smith, for instance, has used his
great literary powers to demonstrate its failure to the
whole world. He has gibbeted Canadian union as a
warning beacon to all constitution-makers of the future.
This view is, however, held by quite a small minority,
and the feeling in favour of federation seems to grow

rather than diminish. The result of the blow dealt at Canadian trade by the United States, by what is known as the M'Kinley Act, is that the Canadians begin to think of bringing Newfoundland and the West Indian Islands into their federal union.

It has been said that a federal union owes its creation to external pressure. There are, however, some instances that do not appear to have originated in this way. Such, for instance, are the Mexican and South American federations, or, again, the Brazilian. The United States of Brazil were certainly not created under pressure. The same may be said of the present tendency to Australian federation. It is conceivable and even probable that, if a serious disagreement arose between the Australian colonies and the mother-country, the colonies would at once unite to present a common front, just as our American colonies did. It is, however, said, on the other hand, that Australian federation is really a step towards Imperial federation, because the Colonial Office would find it much easier to deal with a united Australia than a number of distinct colonies. However that may be, there do appear to be exceptions, where external pressure has had nothing to do with federation. The fact appears to be that the earliest and greatest of federal unions arose in the manner described, but that in subsequent cases federation was adopted as possessing obvious advantages inherent in it quite apart from its origin. Moreover, it must be remembered that it is possible for a federal union to grow up in a converse way from that which has been usual. It may arise from a wish to loosen and not to strengthen a tie. This appears to be the case with Brazil. It has ceased to be a compact and undivided State, and become instead a federal union.

The first condition, therefore, for a federal union is the desire for union without the desire for unity. The problem is, how to carry out this apparently paradoxical desire. And it must be confessed that it is not an easy problem. Some of the federal unions of the world have been preceded by more or less close alliances between the states desiring union, and then the problem is not quite so difficult, because the ground has been to some extent prepared, and the formation of the strictly federal union is only carrying out to its ultimate result a principle already tacitly adopted. This has been the case in Switzerland and Germany. But when there has been no preceding alliance, the case is far otherwise, and we then witness a very striking scene in the drama of national life. We see nothing less than the voluntary abdication by sovereign states of some of the most precious attributes of sovereignty. And this comes about from the very necessity of the problem to be solved. The several sovereign states voluntarily surrender into the hands of another sovereign body that portion of their sovereignty which for the purposes of union they must of necessity surrender. It is true that this sovereign body is the voluntary creation of the several states, but it is a sovereign body none the less. And that portion of their sovereignty that the separate states do surrender is always, at least, that portion which is concerned with foreign relations; such as diplomacy, foreign commerce, questions of peace and war, and naval and military affairs. The separate states desire to present a common external front to foreign powers, so they must of necessity each surrender the conduct of their own foreign relations. What a reluctant surrender this might be can be imagined from the possible creation of a Balkan federation under the pressure of Russia. It would be a bitter pill for such proud states as Bulgaria, Servia, and Montenegro. And after the surrender of the conduct of foreign relations comes sooner or later that of the conduct of internal affairs of common national interest, such as currency, posts, and telegraphs. But the separate states still remain sovereign in everything else. This is well brought out by Article II. of the Constitution of the United States of America: "Every State retains its sovereignty, freedom, and independence." Sovereignty must here mean sovereignty within the limits of the constitution, and not sovereignty in the sense given to the term in International Law.

We now see that a federal government implies a union of several bodies, each sovereign within its own sphere. First, there is the federal union, sovereign within its sphere, which includes, at least, the conduct of foreign relations; secondly, there are the several states, each sovereign within its own sphere. It will be seen, then, that federal union is a matter of contract, and, further than this, that it is a matter of compromise. The architect of a federal union has before him a variety of conflicting forces, some moving in one way, and some in another. His problem is one of social dynamics.

How can he compound these conflicting forces and
make them all move together? The mere statement
of the problem shows its difficulty. "Every great
creation," says M. Rénan, "involves a breach of equili-
brium, a violent state of being which draws it forth."
And this is quite true of the creation of federal constitutions. It is the reason why the Americans look
on their Constitution with such pardonable pride, and
ascribe heroic, almost divine attributes to the founders
of it. "For myself," said Lord Chatham, "I must
declare and avow that in the master states of the world
I know not the people or senate who, in such a com-
plication of difficult circumstances, can stand before
the delegates of America assembled in general congress
in Philadelphia."

These are high words of praise, and may seem
exaggerated, but they are not. The founders of the
American Union solved a great problem with almost
nothing to guide them, and created a federal government which will be the model of all federal governments for the future. The task of any one who had to
construct a federal government was thenceforth comparatively easy, for the constitution of the United
States of America stood as a model. The Brazilians,
for instance, have adopted that constitution almost *en
bloc*. With the founders of the American Constitution
it was far otherwise, for they had few and imperfect
models to follow. But they achieved a remarkable
success, for, notwithstanding the severe trials it has
gone through, the American Constitution still stands
to-day unimpaired,

"And like a surly oak, with storms perplexed,
Grows still the stronger, strongly vexed."

The American Constitution has some grave faults, but it is not too much to say that some of the gravest of them are not by any means necessarily incidental to federal institutions.

We have now seen that the problem is how to adjust aright the claims of conflicting sovereignties. What rights are to be given to the federal union, and what to the separate states? Evidently it must be a matter of compromise, and will vary with the necessities of each case as it arises. The plan adopted in the United States is thus described in the *Federalist:* "The powers delegated by the Constitution to the Federal Government are few and defined. Those which are to remain in the State Governments are numerous and indefinite. The former will be exercised principally in external objects, as war, peace, negotiations, and foreign commerce. The powers reserved to the several States will extend to all the objects which, in the ordinary course of affairs, concern the internal order and prosperity of the State." To put it another way, it may be said that the powers not delegated to the Federal Government nor prohibited to the States are reserved to the States. It may seem a superfluity to expressly forbid the Federal Government to do what it is not authorized to do. Nevertheless the Americans, in excess of caution, did so forbid it. It should be observed, too, that the powers permitted to the Federal Government, but not exercised by it, may be exercised by the States, unless they are expressly forbidden. But these powers cannot be concurrently exercised by both, and the States must always give way to the Federal Government. The various powers in America seem to have been distributed somewhat in this way; some have been given to the Federal Government, others to the State Governments, and yet a third class to both.

In the Canadian Union the powers are distributed in quite a contrary way. The Canadian Constitution confers upon the Dominion Government all powers which are not assigned exclusively to the Provinces, so that, while the American Constitution begins by defining the powers of the Federal Government, the Canadian begins by defining the powers of the separate Provinces. There is nothing capricious in this; on the contrary, it is founded on a sound historical basis. The American colonies were virtually sovereign states coming freely into union, just as the Swiss Cantons were. It was quite natural, therefore, that the semi-sovereign states of America, when they came together, should assign to the Federal Government as few and as well-defined powers as possible. It was natural, too, that they should reserve to themselves as many powers as possible. But the historical growth of the Canadian Union was quite different. The Provinces were not virtually sovereign powers, like the American colonies; they were only divisions of a single colony. Several results flow from the principles of the Canadian Union. First, the central or federal power is much stronger in Canada than it is in the United States. It is much more like that of Germany. It keeps much more in its own hands. It regulates the criminal law and the

law of marriage, appoints the judges and the lieu-
tenant-governors. It controls the militia, and possesses
a veto on provincial legislation. The United States
Federal Government has none of these powers. Then
again it follows that, whilst in the United States the
state rights tend to increase, in Canada the federal
rights tend to increase, because in the one case the
powers of the Federal Government, and, in the other
case, the powers of the separate Provinces, are rigidly
laid down. There is a greater recognition of state
rights in the United States than there is in Canada,
and what is considered to be an inadequate recognition
of state rights is a source of dissatisfaction to some
Canadians. The Honourable Oliver Mowat, the
Premier of Ontario, some few years ago, gave expression to this feeling. The province of Nova Scotia
has a party that threatens cession from the Union
altogether. The distribution of powers, however, must
be made in either the American or Canadian way, or
in some middle course more or less resembling the one
or the other. Switzerland in this respect resembles
Canada rather than the United States, though the
contrary might have been expected.

This distribution being made, the next problem is
what sort of body is the federal government to be, that
body to which the separate sovereignties agree to
surrender powers so important and so valued as the
conduct of foreign affairs, and how are the various con-
tracting states to participate fairly and equitably in the
federal union? This is accomplished by making the
federal government a representative body, the various

elements of which are contributed by the different states. The details vary in each particular case. In the United States the Federal Government is divided very distinctly into three separate authorities — the executive, the legislative, and the judicial. The executive power is invested in the President, who is elected by popularly elected "electors" in each State. The legislative power is vested in the Congress, which consists of the Senate and the House of Representatives. The Senate is elected by the legislatures of the different States, and the House of Representatives by the people in each State. This different mode of election to the Senate and House of Representatives is worthy of note, because in the election to the Senate the principle of the sovereignty of the State is recognized, whereas in the election to the House of Representatives the principle of the sovereignty of the whole people of the United States as a nation is recognized. Lastly, the judicial power is vested in the Supreme Court of the United States, a most important body, of which more will be said hereafter. In Switzerland we see a constitution something like that of the United States, but the executive, legislative, and judicial authorities are not nearly so carefully divided. There the legislative power is vested in a Federal Assembly, consisting of two chambers, a Council of State composed of deputies from each Canton, and a National Council appointed directly by the people. The executive is vested in a Federal Council elected by the Federal Assembly, and presided over by a President. There is also a court which performs some of the functions of the Supreme Court of the United States. The case of the German Empire is peculiar, for it forms at best a very cumbrous form of federation. This, however, is not to be wondered at, in the application of federal institutions to an old country, where local traditions and customs have taken strong root. The head of the German confederation is the King of Prussia, and the post is of course hereditary. Moreover, many of · the separate states are governed by hereditary monarchs. This shows, if proof were needed, that a federal government need not necessarily be republican. This many people are apt hastily to infer from the fact that the United States and Switzerland are republican. There is no reason why federal governments should not be monarchical. Another peculiarity about the German Empire is that all the States are not members of the federation on quite an equal footing. The two states of Bavaria and Wurtemberg have their armies under the commands of their respective kings, except in time of peace, when the German Emperor becomes the Commander-in-Chief of the armies of the entire empire. The Bundesrath and Reichstag, however, are the counterparts of the American Senate and House of Representatives.

The Dominion of Canada is not unlike the United States. The legislative body consists of a Senate, whose members are appointed by the Crown, and a House of Commons elected by popular suffrage. There is a Supreme Court of Canada, which is the counterpart of the Supreme Court of the United States. But there is an appeal from this court to the

British Judicial Committee of the Privy Council.
The executive power is vested in the Queen of Great
Britain and Ireland, and exercised in her name by the
Governor-General. The case of Canada resembles
Germany, in that its head is an hereditary monarch,
but it stands alone (with the exception of the Leeward
Islands) as being at the same time a colony and a
federal union.

We have now seen, from the rough sketch just
given, what are the essential characteristics of a
federal union, and what constitutions the four chief
federal unions of the world have provided to meet the
special difficulties of this form of government. We
are now in a position to note the consequences which
flow from it, and its special difficulties and advantages.
In the first place, we found that federal unions took
their rise for the most part under circumstances of
external pressure. It follows from this that as soon
as the pressure is relaxed, as in many cases must be
the case sooner or later, difficulties will arise; for
the special conditions to meet which the federal
union was formed have vanished. And even in those
cases where external pressure was not the original
moving cause, circumstances may change, and render
union less desirable than it was. Now, it must be
remembered that the federal union was a compromise
between the state rights and the federal rights, and
the probability is that, on the relaxation of pressure,
these rights will come into conflict. One of the
consequences, then, of a federal union is the almost
certain tendency to disintegration, as soon as the

circumstances that gave it birth have ceased to be present. In the language of chemistry, the atoms that make up the federal molecule tend to dissociate. The dissociation may be arrested, but the tendency to it is there nevertheless. This is evidently a dire source of weakness to a federal union. It is nowhere so clearly illustrated as in the history of the United States of America. Even in the time of Washington it was feared that the union would not hold together. Washington himself wrote, " We have probably had too good an opinion of human nature in forming our confederation. Experience has taught us that men will not adopt and carry into execution measures the best calculated for their own good without the intervention of coercive power." In making this remark about having too good an opinion of human nature, Washington touched a weak point in federal unions, for it is the selfishness of the separate states, leading them to prefer state rights to the union made for the common good, which usually helps to wreck federal unions. It may be remarked incidentally that this is one point which shows federal governments to require a high political morality, for unselfishness in the separate states is requisite for its success.

The case of the American union illustrates this. Up to the time of the civil war, there was a continual conflict between state rights and federal rights. Even when not active, the elements of strife were ready at any moment to break out into eruption. So soon after the union as 1786 Massachusetts gave signs of disaffection, and so did Pennsylvania in 1794. In 1812 the States

of Connecticut and Massachusetts refused to obey the
President, when he ordered the militia to march to
the frontiers. In 1832 the Ordinance of Nullification
was passed in South Carolina. All these were shadows
cast before by the coming event of the great civil
war. The fact was that each state was selfish for its
own ¦interests : one wanted slavery abolished, another
wished it retained; one wanted protection, another
free trade.

The case of Switzerland, again, forms a very apt
illustration. This is what Mr. Grote says in his
letters on Swiss politics, written some forty years ago :
" What the Cantons mostly stand chargeable with is
the feeling of cantonal selfishness, each being careless
of the interests of the other Cantons as compared with
its own." We know as a matter of fact that, in the
winter of 1846-47, some of the Swiss Cantons would
not allow provisions to pass their frontiers, although
they knew that, owing to a scarcity of provisions,
there was a starving population in the neighbouring
Cantons. Each Canton preferred its own interests to
that of the common good. M. Druey, the Deputy for
Vaud, expressed the feeling very well when he cited
in the Federal Council the proverb, " My shirt is nearer
to me than my coat." The shirt of cantonal interests
touched the hearts of the Swiss more nearly than the
coat of the federal union. It was even considered
a serious accusation to say that a man was aiming at
unitary and not cantonal government. However, the
result was similar to what occurred in the United
States. There was continual strife; only instead of

its being a question of slavery or no slavery, protection or no protection, it took the form of religious controversy. In 1841 the dispute waxed hot over the right to suppress certain convents in Argau, and the final result was that seven of the Cantons, namely, Lucerne, Fribourg, Schwytz, Unterwalden, Uri, Zug, and Valais, endeavoured to form themselves into a separate federal union, or Sonderbund. And this is exactly what the southern states of America endeavoured to do. In neither case was success attained, and on both sides of the Atlantic the principle of unitary government has triumphed. It has come out of the trial even stronger, just as a fractured bone when set is said to gain resisting power. Nevertheless, disintegration is a danger which has to be reckoned with in every federal union, and there is no good blinding one's eyes to the fact. " Things," said Bishop Butler, " are what they are, and consequences will be what they will be. Why, then, should we desire to be deceived ? " Unless the union is an agreeable one to all parties, or unless secession is allowed, a conflict must inevitably follow, for there can be no peace where opposing interests clash and refuse to harmonize—

> " The children born of these are fire and sword,
> Red ruin, and the breaking up of laws."

In a federal union certain things must happen ; for either the members of the union will prove well-matched yoke-fellows, or they will not. In the first case, the union will, in course of time, become a firmly consolidated and single state; in the second case, it will disintegrate into separate states, either by right

of secession, or *vi et armis;* or, again, although some
of the states may be recalcitrant, yet they may, by the
superior power of the other states, be welded into one
consolidated mass. In a federal union there are, to
use the language of mechanics, two forces at work,
a centrifugal force and a centripetal force. The one
force tends to make the states fly asunder, the other
to drive them together. A federal union may even be
said to be a transitory form of government. It lies
half-way between complete disunion, and complete
consolidation. Disunion will either some day again result, or complete consolidation will be the final development. A federation may be compared, to use a rather
strong metaphor, to Saturn's rings, which seem to be
in a transitory state between disruption into numberless satellites or fusion into one solid mass. In America
it appeared at one time as though disintegration would
gain the day, but now it must be confessed that the
tendency is all the other way. Patrick Henry, carried
away by his ardent nature, exclaimed in Congress more
than a hundred years ago, "All America is fused
into one mass. Where are your landmarks and
boundaries of colonies? They are all thrown down.
The distinction between Virginians, Pennsylvanians,
New Yorkers, and New Englanders exists no more. I
am not a Virginian, but an American!" Patrick
Henry was wrong. All America was very far from
being fused into one mass. The landmarks and
boundaries of colonies were too firmly fixed and deeply
set to be swept away in this easy fashion. But the
words, though said prematurely, may some day be truly

spoken. They are almost true already. Since the civil war, the right of secession has not only been denied, but it is hardly even claimed. That book is, as far as human foresight can go, for ever closed. The American union is, in the words of Chief Justice Chase, "an indestructible union of indestructible states."

As federal governments take their rise under special conditions, it follows that any attempt to create a federal union where these conditions are wanting must most probably end in failure. It has been even said that the success of federal government does not depend upon its own merits, but upon the merits of the race that adopts it. And this is to some extent borne out by facts. The ill success of the federal unions of Mexico, Central and South America, is to some extent due to the fact that federation was inapplicable to the several countries that adopted it. Federation probably lays more doors open to intrigue and corruption than an ordinary single and undivided government. This has been conspicuously the case in the Argentine Republic. Since the revolution there, an examination of the finances of the provinces has revealed a large amount of reckless waste and corruption, and the central government has been compelled to take over their liabilities and the uncompleted public works, which are the nominal security. At the same time, all the political failures of South America cannot fairly be ascribed to federation only. Probably much is due to the inferior aptitude of the Latin races, as compared with the Anglo-Saxon, for democracy. However that may be, federation was probably adopted too rashly in the cases where it has not been altogether successful. It was seen that in the United States federal government worked well, and the American constitution was accordingly copied. Brazil has lately mimicked the United States in the most parrot-like fashion. It elects its President, Senate, and Chamber of Deputies for different periods, it is true, but the only important difference is that the federal district of Rio Janeiro is to be placed exactly on the same footing as any other state or province. This reckless adoption of federal institutions by those for whom it is unsuited, is about as rational a thing as would be the adoption by Morocco of parliamentary government, because parliamentary government works well in England. No constitution can be a success unless it is a natural growth, and in congruity with the particular conditions of the country which adopts it. If borrowed from other and very different sources, it will, like some delicate exotic, fade away and die.

We have seen that the essence of a federal union is a division of powers. Now, this is a palpable source of weakness on the face of it. Divided powers imply always a lack of strength. The powers are divided between the federal government and the state governments. The separate states are always afraid of having their state rights encroached upon by the federal government. This has always been the case in the United States. There from the first there were two parties—the party of state rights, and the party of federal rights. The party of state rights were afraid of the child of their own creation, for, having helped to form the federal government, they dreaded its growing power.

It has been argued by some that the success of the federal governments of the United States and Switzerland shows that the fear of weakness arising from a divided sovereignty is a mere chimera. A moment's consideration will show that this is not so. The United States have not yet been seriously threatened by an external foe, and so they have not yet been put to a severe test. Even the war of independence was carried to a successful issue, not so much by the valour of the colonists as by French assistance and by the difficulties Great Britain had to meet in opposing a foe separated by three thousand miles of ocean. We have already stated that in 1812 the states of Connecticut and Massachusetts refused to obey the orders of the President, acting as Commander-in-Chief of the militia. Such disobedience could only have happened where there was a weak executive. Neither, again, in the case of the war against Mexico, was the United States seriously put to the test. That conflict was a very unequal one, and could have no other issue but victory for the United States. With regard to Switzerland, we know that it has a guaranteed perpetual neutrality. So that, as a matter of fact, it is impossible to say that either the United States or Switzerland have proved themselves to possess a strong executive, and there are strong *primâ facie* reasons for believing that in case of need the executive would be found wanting. It is, perhaps, not too much to say that if the United States

F

had the difficulties to contend with which some European states—France, for instance—have, its constitution could not last a day scarcely. The happy circumstances of the United States, and the political aptitude of its citizens, render it a good workable constitution. Nor is a division of powers the only source of weakness to a federal union. For the separate states are not only jealous of the federal government, but they are jealous of one another. No one state wishes to see any other state or states taking the lion's share in the federal government. In Switzerland it is even provided that the different members of the executive must come from different Cantons. It is obvious from this that it might not improbably happen that Switzerland would be deprived of the services of its most capable citizens. If, for instance, it happened that three of the most capable citizens of Switzerland all belonged to the canton of Zurich, Switzerland would be deprived of the services of two of them. It would be something like this, if Mr. W. H. Smith and Mr. Goschen were forbidden to form part of the same government, because they are both returned by London constituencies.

A further consequence of a division of powers is a tendency of a federal government to split up into coordinate and independent authorities, and therefore there is an uncertainty as to what is the ultimate sovereign body. Something about this has been said in a previous essay, so it must be enough here to note the salient points of the matter. In the United Kingdom of Great Britain and Ireland we know where the ultimate sovereignty is. It is the Imperial Parliament. But in the United States it is not so easy to point out where the ultimate sovereignty really is. It is certainly not in the state legislatures, and it is not in Congress. For Congress may pass a Bill which the Supreme Court may afterwards decide to be *ultra vires* and illegal. The Acts of Congress are legally exactly like bye-laws passed by a local authority. Congress and the Supreme Court are independent and co-ordinate authorities. It is provided by Article V. of the American Constitution, that the Constitution may be amended by the joint action of three-fourths of the States belonging to the union, and ultimate sovereignty must be here if anywhere. In the Canadian Constitution the ultimate sovereignty lies, if anywhere, in the British Crown. These ultimate depositories of sovereign power usually slumber, and are hardly ever invoked. But whether they be the ultimate sovereign powers or not, there can be no doubt of the tendency of sovereign power in federal governments to divide itself into co-ordinate and independent authorities, and this is a source of weakness.

The mention of the Supreme Court brings us to the consideration of another very important consequence of a federal union, and that is the necessity for a strong judicial body. Where powers are divided amongst different bodies, each sovereign within its own limits, it is clear that occasions must arise when the legality of the acts of these different bodies will be called in question. It is also clear that there must be some third independent authority to decide whether the acts called in question are legal or not, and that this body must be a judicial body. This body is, in the United States, the Supreme Court, and a very remarkable court it is, for it is probably the first institution of its kind that history has to show. The Dominion of Canada has a similar court in its Supreme Court, and Switzerland has something like it in its Bundesgericht. But in Switzerland judicial and executive functions are not clearly distinguished, for some points of law are reserved for the consideration of the Federal Council. In no country, except perhaps England, is the judiciary kept so independent of and distinct from the executive and legislature as in the United States. Both in France and Switzerland the legislature claims the right of taking its own view of the constitution, and the Swiss Federal Court is bound to enforce every law of the federal legislature, even though it may consider the law unconstitutional. But quite an opposite state of things exists in the United States. The Supreme Court will declare an Act of Congress *ultra vires* with as little compunction as the High Court in England would in the case of a bye-law passed by some insignificant town council. There is a certain splendour about the Supreme Court of the United States. At its bar we see pleading semi-sovereign and independent states, for it is the function of the Supreme Court to decide questions of the legality or illegality of the acts of bodies sovereign within the limits allowed by the constitution. In this way it comes about that the constitution cannot be understood by a mere perusal of the Articles of the constitution. For the constitution lies as much in the Law Reports of the United States as it lies in the Articles. The United States had the good fortune to have its Supreme Court early presided over by a Chief Justice of pre-eminent strength, and the result is that the name of Chief Justice Marshall must rank along with the names of Hamilton and others as one of the founders of the constitution.

The weakness resulting from a division of powers has already been referred to. But it has been treated, so far, rather from its external than from its internal aspect. There is, however, an internal weakness. Suppose, for instance, a citizen of the United States refused to obey a decree of the Supreme Court. What happens? This is no theoretical difficulty, for it has actually arisen. "John Marshall," said Jackson, "has delivered his judgment; let him now execute it, if he can." This difficulty has been got over largely in the United States by a provision in the constitution that the decrees of the Supreme Court shall affect the individuals that come under the decree personally, not as citizens of this State or that State, but as citizens of the United States, and that the carrying out of the decrees shall be left to the Federal Government, and not to the State governments. A decree of the Supreme Court will run against a man in exactly the same manner in any state whatsoever he may happen to reside. But this is not the whole difficulty, for sometimes a State may support one of its citizens in an attempt to evade a decree of the Supreme Court, or it may itself endeavour to evade such a decree. The only answer to this is that a State acting in this way would be openly in a state of rebellion. No State could venture to act in this way and continue to profess allegiance to the Union. So that whilst on the one hand no individual would dare to defy the whole force of the Union, on the other hand a State would pause long before it committed an act of open rebellion. And in this way the difficulty is rather a theoretical than a practical one. It is worth noticing, however, that in Switzerland the relation of the Federal Government to a rebellious Canton is theoretically different from the relation of the American Federal Government to a rebellious State. The Swiss constitution allows the Federal Government to proceed against the rebellious Canton as a Canton. The American Constitution only allows the Federal Government to proceed against the citizens of a rebellious State as individuals, and not against the State as a State. The State is not considered to be rebellious, but its citizens are. But in both countries the Federal Government is allowed to employ federal troops to suppress disturbances in the various States or Cantons. The Swiss Federal Government lately employed federal troops to suppress a revolution in Ticino.

The advantages and disadvantages of the American federal union have been fully described by Mr. Bryce in his great work on the American Commonwealth; and much of what he says is applicable to federations generally. Some of the disadvantages have already been referred to, namely, the tendencies to weakness in the conduct of foreign affairs and in internal control. One source of weakness in foreign affairs arises from the fact that what may be of vital interest to one member of the union may be of no interest whatever to the other members. A fishery dispute with Great Britain might be of vital importance to a New England State, but of no importance whatever to Nevada or California. Another source of weakness arises from a tendency for states having like interests to combine together. This has actually happened in the case of the New England States, and that of South Carolina and the Gulf States, and it has also happened in Switzerland in the case of the Sonderbund. Such combinations may prove extremely dangerous in cases of war, and they may often lead to secession. A number of states might combine to secede, where a single one would shrink from doing so. A less important disadvantage is the want of uniformity in the law of the component states. No doubt it is disagreeable to be legally married in one state, but to be not legally married when you cross into a neighbouring state. But on the whole the disadvantage is not so great as might be supposed, and it replaces a dull uniformity with a variety which may be both refreshing and instructive. Lastly, there is the trouble, expense, and delay arising from the dual system of government. An American or a Swiss owes a double allegiance to the Federal Government, and to his own particular State or Canton. This is a difficulty, no doubt, but it is not found to be practically important.

On the other hand, federation presents several advantages. First and foremost, it allows of union without unity. It is, indeed, the only institution that can by any means render such a thing possible. Secondly, it gives great facilities for the development of vast territories. Federations need not, it is true, embrace great areas, for Switzerland embraces a very small area. But when applied to great areas it is particularly advantageous. Nothing can be better than the way in which the territories of Western America have been developed and rendered gradually fit to receive self-government. Their example is of happy augury for the future of Australia, should federation there become an accomplished fact. Thirdly, it prevents the growth of central despotic power, and gives opportunities for local self-government. This is an advantage very closely connected with the second. It is clear that where powers are divided between a central government and state governments, the checks put upon the central government at the same time prevent its assuming a despotic position, and leave much freedom of action to the states. And in close connection with this again are the opportunities for legislative experiments. This may of course become an evil if carried to excess, and it is sure to arouse opposition from many. But then, as Luttrell said to Samuel Rogers, "If some very sensible men had been attended to, we should still have been eating acorns." It is one of the advantages of a federal union that it is possible to introduce a novelty in legislation which, if it turns out to be evil, can do no harm outside the limits of one particular state, and which can be easily withdrawn.

There are some peculiarities inherent to a federal constitution which should be noted in conclusion. It should be remembered that a federal union is essentially a contract. Now, it is an elementary proposition of law that a contract should be clearly defined, and have its terms clearly set out. This, of course, can only be done by carefully committing its terms to writing. But anything committed to writing is necessarily rigid. And so it follows that federal constitutions are intensely rigid and conservative. Where there is no written constitution, as is the case in the British Empire, it is far otherwise; all is elasticity. The consequence is that when a change, however small, has to be made in a federal constitution, it can only be done in special ways, and becomes an event of extraordinary importance from the attention it necessarily attracts. But this is not the case where there is no written constitution. Nothing is more extraordinary than the way in which vast constitutional changes have taken place in England almost unawares. Such, for instance, is cabinet government and the present position of the Crown. But in America the constitution cannot be altered a hair's breadth without setting in motion the whole cumbrous machinery for making constitutional changes. Then, again, the fact that a central government and state governments exist side by side prevents the existence of a single capital of the whole union. There is no capital in America, in the same sense that London is capital of England and Paris of France. Washington is only the seat of Congress, but not the capital. New York has in some respects more claim to be called the capital than Washington, but then it is not the seat of Congress. So again in Switzerland, Berne is the seat of the national government, but it is no more the capital than Zurich or Geneva. This absence of a capital operates to prevent the best men from entering the national legislature, because there are none of the advantages offered to them that are presented by residence in a capital city. This is particularly the case in a vast territory like America, where a legislator has to travel enormous distances to attend Congress. Moreover, the co-existence of a central legislature and state legislatures causes a diffusion of political interests. Neither legislature can attract in the way the British Parliament, for instance, attracts. A great sphere of activity and influence is withdrawn from the cognizance and jurisdiction of the federal legislature. And similarly a great sphere is withdrawn from the cognizance and jurisdiction of the state legislatures. And so both are rendered in a large degree uninteresting. This also operates to prevent the best men from entering politics. Then, again, the fact that the entry to the federal legislature lies through the states produces a like tendency. In a large and populous state there may be plenty of men willing and able to represent their state, but they cannot all represent their state at the same time, and they cannot represent any other state. And so it happens that the peculiarities of a federation tend to put political life on a somewhat lower level than in other countries. That this need not be an overmastering necessity is, however, proved by the example of Canada, where the best men do not shrink from politics as they do in the United States. But whatever may be the gains and losses of a federal union, it is clear that they are eminently worthy of attention. At no time in the world's history has federation taken so prominent a place in political institutions as it does at present. It is destined in the future, for good or for ill, to affect multitudes of men.

III.

THE POLITICAL INSTITUTIONS OF SWITZERLAND.

It is said of the inhabitants of Arabia that they are so profoundly ignorant of European affairs that they imagine that all Europeans are of the same race, and that their affairs are arranged by a governing committee of seven kings, who meet together in conference by permission of the Sultan of ·Turkey. Some of them even innocently inquire of travellers whether any Christians are now living. Englishmen are not quite in so bad a case with regard to Switzerland, because so many of them go there in search of health or amusement. But it is surprising how little interest those who do go there take in the people amongst whom they sojourn, and how indifferent they are to any inquiry into their political or social institutions. The great majority of tourists, after spending some months or weeks there, come away with more or less vivid mental pictures of the physical features of the country, but of the conditions of the life of its people they know absolutely nothing. They may thoroughly well know, if they are fortunate in the weather, the

views from the Rigi or the Gorner-Grat, but they have
not the least idea of what takes place in the Parliament
House at Berne. This is unfortunate, because there
is something picturesque in Swiss politics, just as
there is in Swiss mountains and valleys. The political
institutions of Switzerland are indeed peculiarly interesting, and it cannot be doubted but that a knowledge of them would lend some additional flavour
and charm to the delights of a visitor to that pleasant
land.

It is hardly even recognized by many that Switzerland is a federation. Yet it is a fact that, though less
than Ireland both in area and population, it is a union
of no less than twenty-two semi-independent Cantons.
These Cantons, small as they are, are absolutely independent within the limits of the powers granted them
by the constitution, and these powers are considerable.
They have their own legislatures, and make their own
laws. The tiny Canton of Uri occupies a precisely
similar position to the State of New York in America
with its five millions of inhabitants, or to the State of
Texas with its great area of 262,290 square miles.
This may seem extraordinary, but it is true. Moreover, the Swiss federation is really the most ancient
federal union there is. It took its origin in the year
1291, when the men of Uri, Schwyz, and of the Lower
Valley (part of what is now called Unterwalden) combined together to defend themselves against the agents
or bailiffs of the German princes, who held a kind of
feudal sway over Switzerland. This union received
accretions from time to time, the number of Cantons

being made eight in 1353, thirteen in 1513, nineteen in 1803, and finally twenty-two in 1815. The present constitution, which underwent revision in 1874, dates from the year 1848, and, after the United States of America, forms the most perfect of all federal unions. It is true that between 1798 and 1803 Switzerland ceased to be confederation, and was known as the Helvetic Republic. But this was a violent disruption of the natural state of things, and if we leave out of account this short period, as we may well do, we shall see that the Swiss federation has attained the patriarchial age of over six hundred years. It may, therefore, well claim our reverence. But old as it is, it has not despised the modern. On the contrary, it has adopted and assimilated the newest fashions in politics. It has been so thoroughly recast on modern lines that it ranks second to the United States in the logical precision and completeness of its details. Like the British constitution, it has gone on broadening down from precedent to precedent, throwing off the useless and adapting itself to the life of the present. It commands both our reverence and respect, for it combines the dignity of age with the freshness and elasticity of youth.

So much has been said in a previous essay on federal institutions generally, that it would involve much repetition to discuss here the federal union of Switzerland in particular, so that we must pass on to consider some other points in Swiss politics which are no less interesting.

It is not generally known that Switzerland may

fairly claim to be the most democratic country in the world. We are accustomed to think of the United States of America as being the most democratic, but on reflection it must be admitted that this place must be conceded to Switzerland. And this is the more strange because, as a rule, politics in Switzerland pursue the even tenor of their way so quietly that they hardly ever attract outside attention. We sometimes hear of the expulsion of an anarchist or the imprisonment of some imprudent member of the Salvation Army. Quite lately, indeed, a revolution in Ticino has caused a considerable stir, but little more is likely to be heard of it. As a rule we may say of Switzerland, " Happy is the country that has no history; " or, if inclined to be cynical, we might apply to it a remark of Lord Westbury on somebody, that the monotony of his character was unbroken by a single vice. Democracies are generally noisy and blatant. It has been said that while monarchies whisper, democracies bellow. The uproar that the French democracy is capable of creating is only too well known. The French people in a revolutionary humour will raise a clamour loud enough to reverberate over Europe, and set every throne and institution trembling. Again, when anything happens to agitate the people of the United States, we seem to hear the distant rumble of the conflict across the ocean. When, for instance, the American people proceed to elect a President, what a disturbance there is for months beforehand ! How much we hear of the rival claims of this or that candidate ! Or should by some mischance an English

Minister at Washington be led into an indiscretion not to the taste of the American people, what an uproar is raised! How in the eyes of the whole world does the great democracy of the West delight in what it is pleased to call "twisting the lion's tail!" But in Switzerland it is far otherwise. Everything there is done so quietly that hardly any one out of the country knows that they are being done at all. In Switzerland they elect a President annually, instead of every four years as in the United States. Yèt we hear infinitely more of American presidential elections than we do of Swiss ones. Yet, in spite of all this quietness, Switzerland is the only country in the world where we see democracy carried to its extreme and logical results. It is the only country in the world where representative government is backed up and reinforced by an appeal to the people. In other democratic countries, t is only by some elaborate system of checks and balances that it is ensured that a representative government shall truly and really represent the opinion of the majority, and be a reality and not a sham. In England this is done by means of what are called "constitutional conventions." But in Switzerland the whole people can on occasion give their votes individually on some question before the country. This appeal to the people is known as the Referendum. It forms part of the federal constitution, and of most of the constitutions of the several cantons. It is the Referendum which gives the Swiss form of government its extreme democratic character, and, being unique, it is well worth consideration. It is of two kinds—

optional and compulsory. Both kinds have a place in the Federal Constitution. It is compulsory when a question of a revision of the Constitution is before the country. The way in which a revision of the Constitution is introduced and carried out in Switzerland is very remarkable. It is provided that when one of the two chambers of the Federal Assembly, or when fifty thousand voters demand it, then it must be referred to the whole body of voters to say whether the question of revision should be entertained or not. If the voters by a majority affirm the demand, then a Bill for the revision is brought before the Federal Assembly, and this Bill must be referred to the voters again for acceptance. It must be accepted by a majority of the voters and of the Cantons before it becomes law. The Referendum is optional when any Bill or resolution of a general character, not declared to be urgent, is before the Federal Assembly. Then, if thirty thousand citizens or eight Cantons demand it, the proposed Bill or resolution must be referred to the whole body of voters, and it does not become law unless a majority of them accept it. The voters are the electors; and every Swiss who has attained the age of twenty-one years, and who has not been deprived of civil rights, possesses the franchise. From this it will be seen how intensely democratic the Swiss Federal Constitution is. Suppose, for instance, that a poll of the whole British nation—every man of full age having a vote—was taken on the Home Rule question; if we can imagine this being done, it will afford us some idea of the Referendum in Switzerland. It has a place, also, in most of

G

the Cantonal Constitutions. It is compulsory in Zürich, Bern, Solothurn, Grisons, Aargau, Thurgau, Valais, and one of the half-cantons of Basle. It is optional only in Lucerne, Zug, Schaffhausen, St. Gallen, Ticino, Neuchatel, Geneva, and the other half-canton of Basle. The late revolution in Ticino seems to have arisen from the refusal of the Cantonal Council to submit a question of the revision of the constitution to the Referendum after they had been petitioned to do so by ten thousand voters. The Referendum has a very curious effect on Swiss politics. The people know very well that they have in their hands an unfailing weapon and a last resource in the Referendum. The result is that they exhibit a certain apathy and indifference to politics. Moreover, as the law-making lies ultimately in their own hands, they do not mind very much who represents them in the Federal Assembly. So long as the representative is considered a good man of business, they are not much inclined to scrutinize too closely his political colour. It happened some few years ago that, time after time, the people rejected the Bills of the Federal Assembly. They rejected, amongst other things, an Electoral Bill, a Bill on Currency, and a Bill creating a Department of Justice, all of which must have been considered useful measures by the Federal Council. It was naturally thought that the majority in the Federal Assembly did not represent the majority of the people. But at the general election a majority of the same party were returned again. It turned out that the people liked their representatives well enough, but they did not like the Bills that they had brought in. Another result of the Referendum is that it acts as a sort of sedative on popular feeling. When once the Referendum on a particular question has been taken, it is accepted as final, at least for a time, and the decision of the majority is loyally submitted to. The Referendum is very quietly carried out, and it is generally considered by the Swiss that the compulsory kind is better than the optional, because, when it is optional, there is often considerable agitation in debating whether the option should be made use of or not.

The Referendum is so remarkable an institution that it is worth inquiring whether there is anything in other countries at all like it. In England the nearest approach to it is that provision by which the vote of the ratepayers of a parish may be taken on the question whether a rate for creating a free library shall be levied or not. Local option for granting licences would, if adopted, be another instance of the same sort. But this is only the taking of a popular vote for the purpose of deciding whether a particular Act shall be put in operation over a particular area, and not for confirming the passing of the Act itself. In Canada a popular vote is sometimes taken on the question whether a municipality shall financially assist the construction of railways. In the United States of America some of the State Constitutions provide that certain questions shall be submitted to popular vote. Wisconsin, for instance, provides that it shall be referred to the voters to decide whether or not banks shall be chartered. In many local governments of the

United States specific questions are frequently referred
to the popular vote. But all these are like the voting
for a free-library rate in England rather than the
Swiss Referendum. The use that has been made of
the Plébiscite in France has been thought by some to
be the same as the Referendum. But this is not really
so, because the Plébiscite has always been really a
fraud on the French people. They had really no
option but to vote for a particular *régime* that had
been forced upon them. So that the Swiss Referendum
may be fairly said to enjoy the honour of being
a unique institution.

Nor is the Referendum the only powerful weapon of
democracy in Switzerland. In some of the Cantons
there is in operation what is known as the Initiative.
The Initiative is the right of initiating legislation.
This right belongs to the people when a sufficient
number of voters, as fixed by the cantonal constitution,
demands it. The legislative body of the Canton is
bound to introduce legislation when a Bill on a particular subject is demanded by means of the Initiative.
It is found in operation in Solothurn, Grisons, Aargau,
Thurgau, the two half-cantons of Basle, Zug, Schaffhausen, and Neuchatel.

Although the Referendum and the Initiative may
well seem to be the utmost limits of democratic rule,
yet there is a still more democratic institution than
either to be found in Switzerland. This is what is
known as the Landesgemeinden, or the popular assemblies. They are to be found in Uri, the Upper and
Lower Unterwalden, Appenzel, and Glarus. In these

Cantons there is no Referendum, and for a very good reason. It is unnecessary where there is a still more democratic institution already in existence. In the Cantons which we have named, the people do not elect representatives to a governing body, but they meet together themselves in an assembly to conduct their own affairs and make their own laws. This is surely the *ne plus ultra* of democracy, beyond which the most ardent advocate of popular rights could not well go. The Swiss popular assemblies are probably the most ancient political institutions in Europe. It is really a modern instance of that direct legislation by the people which was common enough in antiquity, but which is now excessively rare. Such assemblies are said still to be found in the tiny republics of Andorra and San Marino. They resemble greatly the 'Εκκλησία of Hellas or the Comitia of Rome. There are, indeed, few things in politics more interesting than the Swiss Landesgemeinden. They are more than merely interesting; they are positively heart-stirring and soul-inspiring. For, as Professor Freeman says, in them we look face to face with freedom in its purest and most ancient form. Sir F. O. Adams and Mr. Cunningham, in their admirable volume on the Swiss Confederation, give a most picturesque and graphic description of the Landesgemeinden of Uri. It is impossible to refrain from giving the following short extract:—

"Uri may be taken as an example. There on the first Sunday in May the people assemble in a meadow at Bözlingen an der Gard, not far from Altdorf. The Landamman, after having duly attended mass in the village church, proceeds in procession to the place of meeting. He is accompanied by ushers in antique costumes of black and yellow, the colours of the canton. There is an ancient banner, with the arms of Uri (a bull's head on a yellow ground), and there are old wild bull's horns which year after year are borne upon poles by men in front. The Landamman seats himself at a table in the centre of the meadow, with another official (Landschreiber), and the people, standing or sitting, range themselves around him as in an amphitheatre. The Landamman makes his opening speech, and reviews the events, domestic and foreign, of the previous year. Then there is silence over the whole assembly, every one offering up a prayer, and after that the real business commences. Every man speaks his mind when and for as long as he pleases. Every subject is discussed with decorum, and finally, when all other matters have been settled, the officials for the following year are chosen. The outgoing Landamman (who may be, and generally is, re-elected for another year), delivers up his charge with an affirmation that he has injured no one voluntarily, and he asks pardon of any citizen who may think himself aggrieved. The new Landamman takes the prescribed oath, and the whole people swear to obey him, to serve their country, and respect the laws. Other officials are then elected by a show of hands, and the meeting is over."

These popular assemblies irresistibly remind one of the old Homeric ἀγορά. It is true that in the Homeric ἀγορά the people came together to listen, and not to debate themselves. They did, however, indirectly affect the course of the proceedings by their applause or by keeping a sullen and ominous silence. Mr. Gladstone, in his "Homeric Studies," compares the ἀγορὰ to an English county political meeting. Nevertheless the fact of the ἀγορὰ being an open-air meeting puts it on much the same footing with the Landesgemeinden. The external characteristics are common to both. Then, again, the executive council of the Landesgemeinden stands in much the same relation to those assemblies as the βουλὴ did to the ἀγορὰ. Mr. Gladstone, in his "Homeric Studies," says that "upon the whole the βουλὴ seems to have been a most important auxiliary element of government, sometimes preparing materials for the more public deliberations of the assembly, sometimes entrusted as a kind of executive committee with its confidence." This description makes the βουλὴ not altogether unlike the executive council that conducts the business of those Cantons which have Landesgemeinden. We are tempted to think, too, of the old German assemblies that met together to consider the more important matters, for Tacitus says of the Germans, "de minoribus rebus principes consultant, de majoribus omnes." And so well conducted and orderly are the Swiss that the words applied by Tacitus to the Germans might fairly be applied to them also: "plusque ibi boni mores valent quam alibi bonæ leges." Before leaving the subject of Landesgemeinden, one curious modern instance of a popular assembly should be noted. This is to be found in Norfolk Island, which is a British possession, and is a dependency of New South Wales.

There once annually all male citizens of the age of twenty-five and upwards meet together for the purpose of transacting public business.

When we consider all these elements of democracy, the widely extended franchise, the Referendum, the Initiative, the Landesgemeinden, it will, we think, be admitted that Switzerland is without exception the most democratic country in the world. Rousseau is said to have remarked that a republican form of government is suitable to small states only. Whatever we may think of large states, and whatever aspirations we may have for the future of republican government in large states, it seems clear that there is one conspicuous example of a small state for which a republic has proved itself eminently fitted, and that state is Switzerland. It stands as a reproach to France, and demands at least the respectful regard of the United States.

There is another point in Swiss politics which must be regarded as very democratic, because it is constantly demanded by the Radical party in England, and that is that members of the Federal Assembly are paid for their services. The system must be regarded as democratic because it is found in operation in other democratic countries. In the United States, both senators and representatives receive £1000 per annum, together with tenpence a mile for travelling expenses, and £25 a year for stationery. In Canada and the Australian colonies, the members sometimes of both houses, sometimes of one only, receive payment. In Victoria, members of the Lower House receive £300 a year. In

South Australia, members of both Houses receive £200 a year. In France and a few of the German states members are also paid, but in Italy they are only allowed to travel on the railway free. But the envy of English Radicals would probably be damped if they knew how slender the remuneration of a Swiss member is. Each member receives about sixteen shillings a day for every day he attends during the session, and also about twopence-halfpenny for travelling expenses. Moreover, he does not earn his pay unless he is present when the list of names is called over at the beginning of a sitting, unless he can give some reasonable excuse for his absence. Further, as there are only two sessions a year of about three weeks each, it is tolerably clear that no member can hope to make a living out of political life. Indeed, there is probably no country where so little pecuniary profit can be hoped for from a political career as Switzerland. The Swiss are a very frugal race, and the salaries they offer to their political officers would in this country be considered meagre in the extreme. The President of the Confederation only gets £540 a year, and the Vice-President £480 a year. The Chancellor of the Confederation is rewarded with £440 a year and a house, while the President of the Federal Tribunal, who occupies a similar position to the Chief Justice of the Supreme Court of the United States, only gets £440 a year, and his colleagues on the bench only £400 a year. The length to which economy in administration is carried in Switzerland can be realized when we consider that only a few years ago the people by the Referendum rejected two Bills

of the Federal Assembly for establishing with small
salaries two officials, one in the Chancellor's department, and the other in the Swiss Legation at Washington. As these posts must have been considered necessary by the Federal Assembly and the Federal Council,
it does appear the very extreme of economy for the
people to refuse them. Still, the British Government
Departments might learn a lesson from the Swiss in
this direction, as there appears to be little doubt but
that there is considerable room for saving money in
many of our public offices. There is something salutary,
too, in the arrangements for the sittings of the Swiss
Federal Assembly, which might perhaps be profitably
considered by our members of Parliament. Instead of
meeting in the evening and sitting until the small
hours of the morning, they meet at eight or nine
o'clock a.m., according to the season, and rise at about
one or two o'clock. On Mondays, however, they do
not meet until three in the afternoon, for a reason that
gives us an insight into Swiss homeliness of character.
This hour is fixed in order to allow deputies to return
home after spending their Sundays in their domestic
circles.

And this brings us to consider the Federal Assembly, or what we should call the Houses of Parliament. As in England, there are two houses—the
National Council, which may be said to correspond to
the House of Commons, and the Council of States,
which may be said roughly to correspond to the House
of Lords. A much better comparison is with the
American Congress, which consists of the House of

Representatives and the Senate, corresponding respectively to the National Council and the Council of States. The National Council represents the people, and the Council of States represents the Cantons. There are several points of interest in these two chambers. It is curious, for instance, that while the deputies to the National Council are elected for three years, which is the full term of the existence of any one Federal Assembly, the deputies to the Council of States are elected for no fixed period during that term. They may be elected for the whole of the term or for any portion of it. So that, in a sense, it is the converse of our House of Lords, the members of which sit by hereditary right in each Parliament during its whole existence. Whilst a peer sits for life, a deputy to the Council of States sits only for a short period, sometimes not even during the whole life of the Federal Assembly. Again, the Council of States appears a less important body than the American Senate, for a senator sits for a whole period of six years, for which the Senate is elected, while the House of Representatives is elected for two years only. But although the Council of States differs from the House of Lords and the Senate in these important particulars, it resembles them in others. For instance, there are fewer members of the Council of States than there are of the National Council, just as there are fewer members of the Senate than there are of the House of Representatives. And though the members of the House of Commons are more numerous than the Lords, yet the Lords are in practice usually much the

smaller assembly of the two. Again, the debates
the Council of States are carried on more temperate
and dispassionately than in the National Council.
the former the members address the House sittin
and not standing up, and the debates are carried
more in the manner of a family discussion. T
functions of the two chambers, when considered rel
tively to one another, perhaps more nearly resemb
the relative functions of our Houses of Parliame
than the two American Chambers. They are abs
lutely co-ordinate, whereas the American Senate h
functions which do not belong to the House of Repr
sentatives. For instance, it is the duty of the Senat
and not of the other chamber, to confirm treaties a
official appointments made by the President. It m
be added that the National Council is, in popular es
mation, the more important chamber, because i
members sit for a full period of three years, and n
for a period that may possibly be less. In this superi
importance it resembles our House of Commons.

The Federal Council is one of the most curious a
interesting things in Swiss political institutions, a
stands in singular contrast with the British Cabin
It is, at the same time, like the Cabinet, and yet ve
unlike it. It is a kind of executive committee.
the beginning of every new Federal Assembly, it
elected by the two chambers for the period of the th
years of their own existence. Its President and Vi
President are elected by them annually; so that it
evidently the creature of the Federal Assembly.
this respect it is *primâ facie* very unlike the Briti

Cabinet, which is selected by the Prime Minister, who is requested, in his turn, by the Crown to undertake the formation of a ministry. But this unlikeness is not really so great as it appears, because, in practice, the Crown always selects for its advisers those who command a majority in the House of Commons. The Federal Council consists of seven ministers, who take up different departments of government just as the members of the Cabinet do. But the strange thing about it is that the seven ministers need not be, and in fact never are, of the same political party. They may be, and sometimes are, of diametrically opposite opinions. They form a sort of coalition ministry, a thing which Lord Beaconsfield declared the English detested. Moreover, the Federal Council often contains a majority of a party which is not the same party majority as that in the Federal Assembly. This can best be realized by imagining the Houses of Parliament, containing a Tory majority, electing a cabinet consisting of three Radicals, two Liberals, and two Tories. And what appears stranger still is, that the members of the Federal Council are generally re-elected over and over again, until they resign or die. In this continuity of office they more nearly resemble the English permanent under-secretaries than the Cabinet ministers. The Swiss democracy, at any rate, cannot be accused of fickleness. It seems clear that, in Switzerland, there cannot be much party bitterness, for otherwise such an arrangement as we have described would be impossible. It would be absolutely impossible in France. A ministry composed of Republicans, Royalists, and

Bonapartists would rend itself to pieces. There must also be in Switzerland a considerable amount of feeling of fair play and mutual confidence amongst parties, which politicians of other countries might usefully ponder over. For when a vacancy arises, it is filled up with a due regard that all parties shall be fairly represented. The vacant post does not become a bone of contention, which is immediately fastened on by the party that happens to be in a majority. There is no cry of " the spoils to the victors." When we consider the vehemence of party conflict and the almost delirium of avarice for place that actuates political parties in England and the United States, it is refreshing to turn to Switzerland and see, in actual fact, and as a matter of practice and tradition, the best interests of the country placed before party feeling. Another very peculiar thing about the Federal Council is that its members are not allowed to sit as deputies, or to vote in either chamber of the Federal Assembly. But though they cannot vote, they are allowed to speak. In this respect they are very unlike the British Cabinet ministers. So important is it in England that a Cabinet minister should have a seat in Parliament, that it is considered by his party nothing short of a disaster that he should be defeated at the poll. It would seem strange indeed if our Cabinet ministers were without seats in Parliament, and could not vote there. The Swiss Federal Council, to some extent, resembles the American Secretaries of State, for they have no seats in Congress. But, on the other hand, the American State Secretaries are appointed by the President, and cannot speak or vote in Congress.

There are very considerable merits in the Swiss system of government. It partakes of some of the merits of the American and British systems, and, at the same time, is without some of their defects. In England and France there is a parliamentary government, or government by an executive forming part of the legislature. In America and Prussia there is non-parliamentary government, or government by an executive distinct from the legislature. In the first case, the executive enjoys no independence whatever. It is the creature of the legislature, and lives in its breath. It must either act in harmony with it or perish. In the second case, the executive has independence, indeed, but then it is often in conflict with the legislature. But in Switzerland the executive has independence, and yet is never in conflict with the legislature. In England, the executive, if it runs counter to the majority of the House of Commons, must resign—unless, indeed, believing the country to be at its back, it advises the Crown to dissolve Parliament. In America, Congress may come into bitter conflict with the President, as it did with Andrew Johnson. It cannot get rid of its President. He is elected for four years, and is taken for better or worse. Whatever he does, he will remain in office for that time, unless he commits acts which render him liable to impeachment. But in Switzerland the Federal Council does not resign, if the Federal Assembly does not agree with its policy. Neither does it come into conflict with the Federal Assembly, because it is elected by that body, and represents all shades of opinion. In short, the executive is at once independent and in harmonious relations with the legislature. Nor is this the only merit of the Swiss constitution. It has stability, both constitutional and administrative. It is not every state that has stability of both kinds. The United States, for instance, enjoys constitutional stability in the highest degree. Its constitution is of cast-iron rigidity, and is exceedingly difficult to change. On the other hand, partly owing to the strongly marked separation between the executive and the legislature, and partly owing to a certain dissipation of authority inherent in a federal system, the administration is weak. The troubles in South Carolina, in 1832, and in Kansas, 1855–6, put the executive severely to the test. In France, that laboratory of political experiments, the constitution, though of the rigid type, cannot be called stable. It nearly fell a victim to the machinations of that feeblest of would-be heroes, General Boulanger. It is also administratively weak. It is unusual for a French Cabinet to last for more than a year. But the Swiss constitution is stable, and its administration is independent, fearless, and firm. It suppressed the revolt in Ticino with an admirable promptness.

The position occupied by the President in the federal constitution is interesting. The position of the President of the Swiss confederation probably carries with it less distinction than that of any other head of a state. It is idle to compare him with crowned heads, but it is not uninteresting to contrast his position with that of the presidents of other important republics. The contrast between him and the President of the United States is the most startling of all. There are probably few men who possess such immense powers as the American President. He may not be as powerful as autocratic monarchs, but he is less trammelled than a constitutional monarch. He chooses his own ministers, and can dismiss them at pleasure. He has' the patronage of an immense number of appointments, and has the whole of the executive in his hands. He has a veto over the Bills passed by Congress; he appoints the judges of the Supreme Court, and is Commander-in-Chief of the army. Quite lately he has been invested with quite extraordinary powers under the McKinley Tariff Act. He is empowered to forbid all imports from countries who refuse to admit American cattle after inspection by American inspectors. On the other hand, the Swiss President is little more than a chairman of an executive board. He is only elected for a year. He is even a less important person than the French President, to whom belongs the privilege of neither reigning nor governing. Most educated people could probably in a moment name the French or American Presidents, but how few there are who could give off-hand the name of the Swiss President! This is a very fair test of his insignificance in the eyes of the world. But, though holding this modest position, he occupies an important place in the executive, and does a great amount of very useful work.

The Swiss Federal Council is the only example of a plural executive, or an executive council. When the

architects of the American constitution were discussing
the form their executive was to take, they considered
the Swiss plan of the executive council. As a constitutional king was for them out of the question, they
had the alternative of creating a president or a council.
The latter plan they deliberately rejected, thinking
that party differences in the council might paralyze
the executive authority. Whether or not this would
have been the case in America must always remain
doubtful. But they were probably right. But it is
remarkable that in Switzerland no such paralysis has
ever occurred. In other countries the executive is
really or nominally placed in the hands of one man.
In constitutional monarchies it is placed nominally in
the crown, but really in a popularly elected prime
minister. The monarch reigns, but does not govern.
In the United States it is placed really as well as
nominally in the President. He governs, but does not
reign. In France it is placed nominally in the
President, but really in a popularly elected prime
minister. The French President neither reigns nor
governs. In autocracies it is placed really and
nominally in the monarch, who both reigns and
governs. There are, indeed, other conceivable forms
of the executive. The King of Sweden, for instance,
has partly the position of a constitutional monarch,
and partly the position of a president of the American
type. The old elective Kings of Poland and the
Doges of Venice had a somewhat similar position.
But they were rather monarchs than presidents. In
Switzerland alone do we find the executive, so to

speak, placed in commission. The Federal Council (and not its President) occupies the position of a monarch or a president in other countries. The Swiss constitution, therefore, offers but little scope for the abilities of its President. It provides no room for a Washington or a Lincoln. Neither, on the other hand, does the mode of election lead to the choice of such mediocrities as a Polk or a Pierce. Both in America and France it is often dangerous to elect the best man. As was long ago said by Swift, the quality of being the fittest is fatal to any candidate. The best man is often the worst candidate. In the last French presidential election M. Carnot was elected. He was not, however, nearly so well known as M. Freycinet, M. Jules Ferry, or M. Floquet. But he divided parties least. The Swiss President is almost sure to be the best man for the post, but the best man for the Swiss presidency is not the brilliant orator or forger of great ideas in policy, but merely one who can best carry on the ordinary affairs of government in a business-like way.

The political institutions of Switzerland are well worth studying. They are in many ways interesting, and at least in one point, the Referendum, unique. Then, again, what is there in modern political life at all comparable for picturesque colouring and dramatic action with the Landesgemeinden? The Federal Council again, both in its constituent elements and its relations to the Federal Assembly, presents many interesting points, and stands in remarkable contrast with the British Cabinet system. Swiss political life,

too, has in some ways reached an almost ideal rectitude
and loftiness, and must stand as an example and a
model to other countries. There is probably no
country where party feeling is so much subordinated
to patriotism, or where there is less political bitterness.
There are few statesmen who do so much hard and
honest work for so little reward as the men who form
the Swiss executive. Altogether the impression left
upon the mind of the student is that the Swiss deserve
well of fate, and that there is a purity and loftiness in
their life and character which harmonizes well with
the eternal snows of the mountains, the limpid streams
and lucid lakes, amongst which they live.

IV.

THE PROGRESS OF THE "MASSES."

NOTHING so much exercises the mind of many at the present time as the social questions arising from the unequal distribution of wealth. The causes to which this fact may be ascribed are mixed, and it is difficult to say which has been the most powerful. First, there is the extension of the franchise, and the consequent increased power of the people to make their voices heard; secondly, and closely connected with this, is the readiness of political agitators to find out real grievances or invent imaginary ones for the newly-enfranchised—the mob service, in short, of the courtiers of the people; thirdly, there is the growth of education, which, as a great writer. has said, "is not the equalizer, but the discerner of men;" and directly consequent upon education is the quickening of the imaginative faculty, that "mighty priest and prophet to lead us heavenward, or magician and wizard to lead us hellward." And directly consequent upon the larger imaginative faculty (and through it upon education) is the increased power of sympathy, "the universal solvent" that eats away the barriers dividing man from man and class from class.

Whatever the causes, the facts are patent, and it would be easy to indicate, did space allow, the extent to which social questions are "in the air," producing in some that pessimistic spirit which wrung from the lips of the great Lord Shaftesbury, shortly before his death, the saddening remark that he did not like to leave the world with so much misery in it. Yet there are many hopeful signs in the situation which any one who will admit the cogency of facts and figures must be compelled to admit.

And first of all, a rapid glance at the history of the labour question will teach us that the labouring classes have only recently emerged from a state of slavery.

The very word "servant" suggests slave by its derivation. "It is familiar," says Mr. W. O. Holmes in his treatise on the Common Law, "that the status of a servant maintains many marks of the time when he was a slave. The liability of the master for his torts is one instance."

We hear much of liberty in this country; we boast of it; our historians laud it, and tell in impassioned words by what manner of men and by what efforts and self-sacrifices it was won; our philosophers write treatises upon it, and our poets dedicate odes and sonnets in its honour. Yet this much-glorified liberty, valuable though it is, is liberty in the political sense only; and as, in the words of Hobbes, political liberty is political power, the liberty we praise is the power to participate in government, and the struggles by which that power was gained were the struggles made in removing the restraints that forbade men to grasp it. Yet all this time liberty, in the fuller and truer sense of the word—that is to say, liberty of the person —was comparatively neglected. This liberty of the person has been classed by philosophers and jurists among "primordial" or "natural" rights. Yet from the way in which it has been regarded one would rather be inclined to say that, so far from being "primordial," it was one of the last rights to be granted to suffering humanity. It is a remarkable thing how men have fought and suffered for political liberty, while they have only lightly estimated personal and individual liberty. The Athenians, who commemorated in song Harmodius and Aristogeiton, exhibited a callous indifference to the great slave population bowed down beneath their yoke. Brutus, in his love of political liberty, stayed not his hand from the murder of Cæsar, but raised not a finger to relieve the numberless slaves that formed so large a part of Roman society. When Thrasea Pœtus opened his veins, and as the blood flowed cried, "I pour a libation to Jupiter the Deliverer," he had in his mind the deliverer from political tyranny rather than the deliverer from the tyranny of the slave-master. Indeed, we cannot help saying with Hallam, that "we lose a good deal of sympathy with the spirit of freedom in Greece and Rome when the importunate recollection occurs to us of the tasks and the punishments which might be inflicted, without control either of law or opinion, by the keenest patriot of the Comitia or

the Council of the Five Thousand." When Rousseau
said that man was born free, but was everywhere in
chains, he was thinking chiefly of the reign of the few,
for which he wished to substitute the rule of the
people. The descendants of those Catholics who,
flying persecution at home, sought religious liberty
in another clime, and founded the States of Maryland
and Virginia, did not hesitate to impose on the negro
a yoke of slavery far more cruel than any oppression
their ancestors had suffered. Nay, more; during the
Civil War in America a large number of Englishmen
were found to express their sympathies with the slave-
holding states of the South. Of them J. S. Mill remarked that their action disclosed "a mental state in
the leading portion of our higher and middle classes
which it is melancholy to see, and will be a lasting
blot in English history." It is indeed remarkable
that Englishmen who had unbounded admiration for
their forefathers, who had done so much in the cause
of political and religious liberty, should have looked
with sympathy on those who were endeavouring to
perpetuate an institution which denied the boon of
personal liberty. But we revere the memories of Pym
and Hampden more than those of Clarkson and Wilber-
force.

We have remarked that it is only comparatively
recently that the condition of the labourer has approxi-
mated to freedom. It is indeed too true that slavery
has been the almost universal custom of the human
race. That all the ancient civilizations were slave-
holding states is notorious; the flight of the slaves

from Athens during the Peloponnesian war, the cruel
murder of the Helots in Sparta, and the cold and
callous way in which the Greek philosopher spoke of
the slave as a living tool, testify to the extent of
slavery in Greece. The ruinous system of "ergastula,"
the provisions of the Roman law, which hardly raised
the slave above the position of the domestic animal
(for it was not until the reign of Antoninus Pius that
it became homicide to kill a slave), the Servile War,
are a few examples out of many that show the magni-
tude of slavery as a Roman institution. The pyramids
raised by the bloody sweat of tens of thousands beneath
the lash are an everlasting monument of Egyptian
bondage; and we need scarcely be reminded of the
Israelites, whose lives the Pharaohs made "bitter with
hard bondage in mortar and in brick, and in all
manner of service in the field." These examples,
taken at random out of many, must suffice to show
how widespread and terrible was the curse of slavery
in the Old World states. Well might St. Paul divide
men into bond and free!

In the Dark and Middle Ages things were scarcely
better. The Roman Empire has been described by
Mr. John Morley as a vast imperial state with slavery
for a base. The word "slave" is a bit of fossil history.
It tells us that the Slavs were reduced to the condition
suggested by the word "slave." Christianity, it is true,
by inculcating the duty of manumission, did something to ameliorate the hard lot of the slave, but so
late as the seventh century Pope Gregory the Great
was constrained by his sympathies to do what he could

to wipe out an institution so incompatible with the precepts of his faith. Mrs. Jameson, in her work on the Monastic Orders, relates a beautiful story of St. Baron and his enfranchised slave. That the lowest ignominy, the lash, and the prison, were the lot of the slave in the seventh century it eloquently and pathetically testifies. "Throughout these ages," says Hallam, "servitude under somewhat different modes was extremely common." Besides slavery in its most absolute form, there were various degrees of serfdom and villeinage. In England, in the reign of Henry the Second, there was a class of villeins who could hold no property and were destitute of all means of redress; and so late as the reign of Elizabeth predial servitude undoubtedly existed. In France predial servitude existed down to the very days of the Revolution; and La Bruyère, in glowing and impassioned words, speaks of "certain wild animals, male and female, scattered over the fields, black, livid, all burnt by the sun, bound to the earth that they did till with unconquerable pertinacity; they have a sort of articulate voice, and when they rise on their feet they show a human face, and are in fact men."

Confining our attention to England, we find that by degrees serfs and villeins developed into hired labourers, but that the legislators did what they could to render their freedom a mockery. This is well shown by what happened after the dreadful pestilence of 1348, which greatly reduced the number of labourers, and consequently enhanced the price of labour. What happened was the passing of the famous Statute of Labourers, which J. S. Mill justly says was intended to prevent the labouring classes from taking advantage of diminished competition to obtain higher wages. "Such laws," he says, "exhibit the infernal spirit of the slave-master, when to retain the working classes in avowed slavery has ceased to be practicable." By this statute, passed in the year 1350, it was exacted that every man in England, of whatever condition, bond or free, of able body and within sixty years of age, not living of his own or by any trade, should be obliged when required to serve any master who was willing to hire him at such wages as were usually paid three years before. The price of labour was actually fixed, and no more than the old wages was allowed to be given or asked for. The labourer, too, was forbidden to leave the parish in which he lived in search of better-paid employment. A law more oppressive to the labourer can hardly be imagined. That it ended in the great Peasant Revolt cannot be wondered at. We can well understand in what spirit the burning words of John Ball, the mad priest of Kent, would be received—words in which he contrasted the lives of the employer and the employed: "They are clothed in velvet, and warm in their furs and ermine; while we are covered with rags. They have wine and spices and fair bread; and we oat-cake and straw, and water to drink. They have leisure and fine houses; and we have pain and labour, the rain and the wind in the fields. And yet it is of us and of our toil that these men hold their state." They might well have echoed the despairing words of the Hebrew preacher, that there was no profit in their labour under the sun. Nor was this the only statute enacted in order to restrict the freedom of the labourer. By a statute passed in the twelfth year of the reign of Richard the Second, no servant or labourer could depart, even at the expiration of his service, from the hundred in which he lived, without permission under the King's seal; nor might any one who had been bred to husbandry up to the age of twelve years exercise any other calling. By a statute passed in the seventh year of the reign of Henry the Fourth, any one who did not possess a certain property qualification was forbidden to put his son or daughter as an apprentice to any trade in a borough, and the House of Commons about the same time unsuccessfully attempted to prevent villeins sending their children to school. So beneficent was the rule of a Government of employers! They had yet to learn the truth of the inscription on the tomb of Bahran-gor: "The hand of Liberality is stronger than the arm of Power." These statutes affected chiefly the agricultural labourer; but the artisan of the town fared but little better. In the fifth year of the reign of Elizabeth was passed the famous Statute of Apprentices, which almost equals the Statute of Labourers in its oppressive restraints. By this statute justices of the peace were enabled to fix the rate of wages; artisans were compelled to remain in the same trade in which they were apprenticed, and were only allowed to leave the place in which they lived under certain conditions; a fixed number (a minimum, not a maximum) of hours for work was imposed; women might be compelled to enter into service. These were some of the provisions of the Act. Fortunately for this country it was judiciously decided that its provisions only applied to trades actually existing at the time of the passing of the Act, and not to newly discovered occupations. So long as agriculture was the staple employment of the people, the sphere of the operation of the statute was comparatively small, but with the growth of this country as a manufacturing and mercantile community it became much more important. From time to time it was supplemented by statutes passed to regulate the rate of wages and hours of labour in particular trades. For instance, in 1720 a statute was passed to regulate journeymen tailors; in 1725 the wool-makers, in 1749 the hat-makers, in 1777 the silk-weavers, in 1795 the paper-makers, were respectively made the subject of similar legislation. In 1799 a general Act, following similar Acts of the reigns of Edward the Sixth and Charles the Second, was passed to suppress combinations to force an increase in wages. By this time the question of the legality of such combinations had become very important, and in the years 1800, 1824, 1825, and 1871, the Legislature made various attempts to deal with it, and it was not until 1875 that it was put on a satisfactory footing by the Conspiracy and Protection of Property Act. It was not until then that the spirit of the old Statute of Apprentices was finally eradicated.

During the latter part of the last century the invention of the spinning-jenny and the mule and that of the steam-engine began an industrial revolution that completely altered the condition of the English labourer. With the growth of factories a new class of workmen arose into importance. In two directions the introduction of the spinning factory worked at first to the disadvantage of the labourer. In the first place, the agricultural labourer suffered; and in this way: Formerly it was customary for the family of the peasant to eke out their small wages by working at the spinning-loom at home. After the introduction of the spinning factory this form of domestic labour became no longer profitable, and the wages of the peasant remaining as low as before, his condition became more wretched than ever. In the next place, the introduction of the factory system enabled the factory owner to exercise over the operatives in his employ a power that was often oppressive. The reader of Lord Beaconsfield's "Sybil" will remember the graphic words in which he described what he felt to be at once a danger and a disgrace. During the early part of this century in England the condition of the working classes was indeed a wretched one. The late Mr. Arnold Toynbee, in one of his lectures delivered in London, in St. Andrew's Hall, Newman Street, in 1883, stated that it is well known by those qualified to judge, that the condition of the workmen in England was one of civilization compared to what it was forty years ago. He tells us to turn to the memoirs of the Chartists, Samuel Lovett and Thomas Cooper, to read of men who clamoured to be sent to prison that they might not starve, and of labourers

who burnt ricks, and asked when the fighting was to
begin. The lot of humanity has been tersely described
in these words: "They are born; they are wretched;
they die." And indeed, when we direct the light of
history down the corridors of time, and look into the
obscure nooks and crannies—when we look beneath
the tinsel of courts and princes, and the glamour of
wars, that make up so large a part of history, a state
of things is disclosed to us that constrains us to believe
that this has often been a too accurate description.
When one thinks of these things it becomes easy to
understand how men of keen sympathies, men like St.
Simon, Fourier, and Karl Marx, should have devoted
their labour and their genius to devising systems for
readjusting and recasting society.

But with the present century, and more particularly
during the last fifty years, a brighter day has dawned
for the labourer. The misery indeed that darkened
the first part of this century was a shadow thrown by
a relentless fate, rather than the offspring of legislative
oppression. It was one of those cataclysms like an
earthquake, or a plague, that occasionally overwhelm
society. The remark of the Persian writer, that the
angel who presides over the storehouse of the winds
feels no compunction though he extinguishes the old
woman's lamp, seems applicable to a time when the
hand of Fate fell heavily on the poor and helpless.
If we except only the corn laws, of which Sir E. May
says that in order to ensure high rents it was decreed
that multitudes should hunger, the misery was engen-
dered by causes that were inevitable. The revolution

in the methods of labour that always follows the introduction of machinery, combined with a number of bad
harvests and the Napoleonic wars on the Continent,
and the consequent scarcity of food, to cause all the
misery. But for all this, with the beginning of the
century the seed of a veritable revolution in the position
of the labourer, at least in England, began to be sown,
and since then his condition has steadily improved.
This improvement may be traced in a variety of ways.
First, let us take the legislative measures passed
expressly to assist the labouring-classes. Formerly
the legislator only busied himself, if he thought of the
working man at all, with devising means of putting
restraints on the rights of the workman. The Statute
Book was disfigured with such statutes as the Statute
of Labourers and the Statute of Apprentices. But
during the present century the legislator has wearied
himself, with an ever-increasing activity, to cram the
Statute Book with laws of real or supposed advantage
to the labourer. It is as though, smitten by remorse
and lashed by the scourge of an avenging conscience,
he was impelled to make haste to redress the wrongs
of centuries. The statutes passed to regulate labour
in factories alone occupy a considerable space. Beginning with the year 1802 we have the Health and
Morals Act, 42 Geo. III. c. 73. Then we have the
following series of Factory Acts :—59 Geo. III. c. 66 ;
6 Geo. IV. c. 63 ; 1 & 2 Will. IV. c. 39 ; 3 & 4 Will. IV.
c. 103 ; 5 & 6 Vict. c. 99 ; 7 & 8 Vict. c. 15 ; 13 & 14
Vict. c. 54 ; 23 & 24 Vict. c. 78 ; 30 & 31 Vict. c. 103 ;
30 & 31 Vict. c. 146 ; 37 & 38 Vict. c. 44 ; 41 & 42 Vict.

c. 16. In the year 1842 an Act was passed prohibiting women and girls from working in mines or collieries. In addition to these Acts we have had many other Acts passed to assist the labourer. There is the Truck Act, 1 & 2 Will. IV. c. 37 ; the Act to secure the payment of wages without stoppages in the hosiery manufacture, 37 & 38 Vict. c. 48; the Merchant Shipping Payment of Wages Act, 43 & 44 Vict. c. 16. The various Combination Laws and the Conspiracy and Protection of Property Act we have already referred to. Then there is the Trades Union Act, 1871, and the Employer and Workmen Bill, 38 & 39 Vict. c. 90; the Employers' Liability Act, 43 & 44 Vict. 42, and the alterations in the Law of Partnership made to render Co-operative Societies possible. Then there are the Acts relative to the Housing of the Working-Classes, namely : the Housing of the Poor Act, 1868 ; the Housing of the Poor Act, 1875 ; the Artisans' Dwellings Amendment Act, 1879. The agitation with reference to the hours of labour in shops must be fresh in the minds of every one. Then, again, there are a series of Acts relating more particularly to sailors, namely : the Unseaworthy Ships Bills of 1878 and 1882, and the Merchant Shipping Bills of 1871, 1872, and 1876. The Friendly Society Act, 1875, and the Education Act, 1870, may be said to have been passed more particularly for the working classes than any others. Amongst other Acts passed in favour of the labourer may be mentioned the Public Libraries Act, 1866, and the Cheap Trains Act, 1883. These Acts, it will have been observed, relate almost, if not entirely, to the artisan and factory

I

classes, and not to the agricultural labourer. He has been neglected in comparison with his brethren in the towns; but amongst Acts affecting him may be named the Agricultural Gangs Act, 30 & 31 Vict. c. 30, and the Agricultural Children Act, 1873.

Two series of measures which perhaps more than anything else have ameliorated the condition of the poor remain to be mentioned; first, the Acts repealing the import duties on corn and other articles of food; and, secondly, the Acts extending the franchise. The first have bestowed cheap food, and the second increased Parliamentary representation; and, taken alone, they mark a great advance.

It was the great mission of Sir Robert Peel to in-augurate freedom of trade. Between 1842 and 1846 he repealed altogether the duties on about five or six hundred articles, and reduced them on a good many articles besides. Then came the repeal of the Corn Laws, and with it the certainty of cheap bread. In 1853 Mr. Gladstone repealed many duties, including that on soap, and reduced those on many other articles, including tea and fruits, and in 1861 that on paper; and this policy he continued, so that, whereas in 1842 there were 1052 articles subject to import duty, by the Budget of 1860 the number of such articles was finally reduced to forty-eight. And though it may be said that all classes have benefited by the consequent lowering of prices, yet the poor undoubtedly have benefited the most by a fall in price of the necessaries of life. Of the extension of the franchise it will be enough to note its initiation in 1832, and its final stage reached in 1884.

We have seen in what a variety of ways the Legislature has within the present century been active to remove the grievances of the working-classes. This agency of the Legislature may be classed as one working from without. Let us now turn our attention to one of a more spontaneous character, for it surely must be deemed a step in advance that the working-classes have learnt to take an independent standpoint.

The agencies of this character may be described as regulated self-help. The working-classes have undeniably combined together to help themselves, and have succeeded in some respects in a remarkable degree. It is true that they have received some Government assistance in the alterations of the law, which have rendered trades unions, co-operation, and the investment of savings possible. Still, the broad fact remains, that the working-classes have done much to aid themselves; and this they have done chiefly in the three ways already briefly indicated—namely, by the creation of trades unions, of co-operative societies, and the investments of savings. And of these three, co-operation has been by far the most successful, and merits special attention.

Co-operation has had a remarkable history in England. So far back as the year 1777 we hear of a co-operative workshop of tailors at Birmingham, and we know that Barrington, the Bishop of Durham, in 1795 set up co-operative stores at Mongewell, in Oxfordshire. In 1816 the "Economical Society" was formed at Sheerness. During the early part of the century, too, Owen established the principle of co-operation amongst his workmen at Lanark with much success. By the time the year 1830 was reached as many as over 300 co-operative stores were set up in different parts of the country ; but, owing to the then state of the law relating to limited liability and defective management, many of them failed. In 1844 the Society of Rochdale Pioneers came into being, and from small beginnings it has developed to remarkable proportions, and given an impetus to co-operation all over the country. In the first year of its existence its members numbered 28, and no profits were made ; whilst in 1876 they numbered 8892, and the profits amounted to £50,000. Rochdale took the lead, but other towns soon followed. The co-operative stores at Leeds, for instance, had in 1886 no less than 23,000 members, and in that year made profits of £59,000 ; while the two co-operative societies at Oldham in 1886 had between them about 23,000 members, and made a profit to the amount of £90,000. These are some of the largest and most successful of co-operative societies, but the extent to which the movement has spread amongst the labouring population can only be estimated by looking at it in the aggregate all over the country. Taking England first, we find Lancashire leading with 196 societies, and Yorkshire second with 187 ; the total number in England is 591, with 674,602 members, making profits to the amount of £2,331,055. Taking Scotland next, we find that Lanark leads with 64 societies, the total number in Scotland being 305, making profits to the amount of £523,823. Next comes Wales with 23 societies, making profits to the

extent of £26,580. And lastly, Ireland, with nine
societies, making profits to the amount of £2008.
Altogether, co-operative stores in Great Britain and
Ireland number about 12,000, with 900,000 members,
receiving a total profit of £2,500,000. Such are the
figures returned for the year 1886, and no one can
deny that they exhibit a capacity for self-help and for
union, a self-reliance and a thriftiness, which mark
a distinct advance in the condition of the masses.
They are no longer, one and all, isolated and helpless
units, as they were a hundred years ago, but many of
them form a strong phalanx, united both in heart
and mind, and sustained by considerable pecuniary
resources.

The next form of regulated self-help that claims our
attention is trades unionism. Here again we can mark
a great improvement in the condition of the masses.
It is true that trades unions, by ill-judged strikes and
by indefensible actions, have at times hindered rather
than advanced their cause. Yet on the whole they
have enabled the labourer to be no longer at the
mercy of the employer, and in so far as they take the
form of provident societies they have stimulated thrift
and self-dependence.

Another form of regulated self-help is the saving of
money by investments in the savings-banks. Investment of savings is not merely in itself an advance, but
it indicates an advance by showing that the amount of
wages received is large enough to allow a surplus
beyond what is spent in obtaining a bare subsistence.
It must not be forgotten, too, that a saving of money

must have been made in order to support trades unions and co-operative societies. But here we are particularly concerned with savings - banks. Government assistance must also here be recognized. It was in the year 1817 when saving-banks first received Government recognition, and in 1827 and 1828 they received further Government assistance. The amount of money saved, and the rapidly increasing way in which it has been saved, will be made apparent by a glance at the following figures, which are given on the authority of Professor Leone Levi: In the year 1831 the capital of savings-banks in England amounted to £13,719,495; in 1841 to £24,475,000; in the year 1850 to £28,931,000; and in 1878, taking into account the sums deposited in Post Office Savings-Banks, to £74,705,000. These figures speak for themselves.

We have now spoken of legislation and regulated self-help. There yet remains a third way of estimating the progress of the people, and that is by estimating and comparing the amount of wages received formerly and now, and by estimating and comparing the effective or purchasing power of those wages; that is to say, their real, and not merely their money value. This can be done only by examining the history of prices side by side with the history of wages. This it is possible to do with more or less accuracy at various periods in English history; and though statistics are often repellant, here at least they will repay perusal.

Professor Rogers has investigated carefully the wages and prices prevailing in our earlier times, and he has arrived at the following figures for the thirteenth

century. Taking agricultural labourers first, he finds
that the average wage for a man was 2d. per day ; for
a woman, 1d. per day; and for a boy, ½d. per day.
Allowing for deductions for Sundays and holidays, the
total wages for a man is estimated at £2 11s. 8d. per
year. But during harvest-time wages were doubled,
so that the total wages for a man may be put down at
£2 15s. a year. Sometimes a hind was hired for a
whole year, and paid by receiving a quarter of corn
(valued at 4s.) every eight weeks, and 6s. in money.
This would amount to £1 12s. a year; and if he was
boarded, as was sometimes the case at harvest and
exceptionally busy times, reckoning the cost of board
at 1½d. a day for six weeks, the total wages would
amount to £1 15s. 8d. a year. The wages of artisans
for the same period next claims our attention. Taking
carpenters, for example, we find that on the average
they received from 3d. to 3½d. a day, and that a pair of
sawyers received 7d. a day, and sometimes more. At
the building of Newgate Gaol, in 1281, the carpenters
received 4d. to 5½d. a day; the sawyers, 9½d. a day;
and the masons, 5d. a day. Professor Rogers estimates
the average wages of artisans in the thirteenth century
at £4 7s. 6d. a year in the provinces ; and in London,
where wages were higher, at £6 17s. 6d. a year. Then
as to prices, in order to avoid the burden of figures, it
will be enough to quote Professor Rogers, who says
that "all necessaries in life in ordinary years, when
there was no dearth, were abundant and cheap," and
to note that the average price of wheat from 1261 to
1340 was 5s. 11¼d. a quarter, ranging from 2s. 10½d. to

16s. a quarter. In ordinary years the price ranged from 4s. 6d. to 6s. 6d. a quarter.

Let us next take the period from the year 1400 to 1545, which Professor Rogers calls " the golden age " for the English labourer. He says that at this period an ordinary artisan would get 6d. a day, and an agricultural labourer 4d. a day ; and in the year 1495 he calculates that an agricultural labourer could earn at the then prices three quarters of wheat, three quarters of malt, and two quarters of oatmeal by fifteen weeks' work, and that the artisan could earn the same by ten weeks' work. From this time onward prices began to rise, so that in the year 1564 Professor Rogers calculates that it would take the agricultural labourer forty weeks, and the artisan thirty-two weeks, to earn the same quantities as they did in 1495, while in 1593 not a whole year's labour would suffice.

In 1597 and 1610 things were much worse even than this. We have the authority of Sir W. Petty for a statement of the rate of wages for the seventeenth century. He puts down the wages of the agricultural labourer at 4d. a day with food, and 6d. a day without food. During the latter half of this century we find the justices of Warwickshire fixing the rate of wages at 4s. a week without food, except from September to March, when it was 3s. 6d. In 1682 the justices of Suffolk fixed them at 5s. a week without food in winter, and 6s. without food in summer; and in 1661 the justices of Essex fixed them at 6s. a week without food in winter, and 7s. without food in summer. At this time, too, the workmen employed in manufactures received not more than 1s. a day, and often only 6d. a day. When we consider that the average price of corn from 1673 to 1685 was 50s. a quarter, it will be apparent that the wages of the labourer had much less purchasing power than they once had.

For the latter part of the eighteenth century we are indebted for some valuable figures to Arthur Young. Speaking of about the year 1767, he put the wages of agricultural labourers at the rate of £18 per annum in Hertfordshire, and £17 in Northamptonshire and Derbyshire; whilst with regard to artisans, taking various trades, he puts the wages of colliers at 15s. a week; of ironworkers, at 13s. 6d. a week; of porcelain-makers, at 9s. 6d. a week; of weavers, at 10s. a week; of wool-combers, at 12s. a week; of carpet-makers, at 12s. a week; of pen-makers, at 15s. a week; of steel-polishers (at Woodstock), at 42s. a week; and of blanket-makers, at 12s. a week. Then as to prices: he puts bread at 1¼d. a pound, butter at 6½d., cheese at 3½d., and meat at 3¾d. a pound. But after the year 1780 wheat was hardly ever below 50s. a quarter, and in 1795 it was double that price.

Coming now to the present century, we know very well that during the early part of it the condition of the agricultural labourer was miserable—how miserable we may infer from the statement of Mr. Giffen, that the agricultural labourer's wages have risen 60 per cent. since the period before the corn laws. A considerable rise in his wages has taken place since 1860, for in that year they were (according to Professor Leone Levi) 8s. 8d. a week in Kent and 15s. in Cumberland; while in 1872 they were 26s. in Kent and 20s. in Cumberland. Nor was the condition of the factory hand any better, if we may judge from the wages of the weavers, who, though in 1802 they received as much as 13s. a week, in 1817 only received 4s. 3½d. a week. It must be borne in mind, too, that during the early part of this century the price of wheat was abnormally high. In the year 1801 it touched the enormous price of 156s. 2d. a quarter, and from 1800 to 1820 it averaged 98s. 6d. the quarter.

During the last fifty years there has been a contemporaneous increase of wages and decrease of the prices of commodities. In the case of carpenters, bricklayers, masons, miners, weavers, and spinners, Mr. Giffen estimates the rise since 1826 at over 50 per cent. in most cases and at over 100 per cent. in some. In the case of seamen's wages, he estimates the rise since 1850 at 60 per cent., and in the case of agricultural labourers, since the time preceding the repeal of the corn laws, at 60 per cent. Taking particular trades, we find, on the authority of Professor Leone Levi, that hands in cotton factories who in 1839 received 7s. and 16s. a week respectively, in 1877 received 17s. 6d. and 36s.; that hands in woollen factories, who in 1837 received 12s. and 21s. a week respectively, in 1877 received 35s. and 28s.; that whilst in the linen trade in 1855 some hands received only 10d. and 4s. a week respectively, the same class in 1877 received 8s. and 33s.; that in the earthenware trade, between 1857 and 1877 there was a rise from 3s. 6d. a week to 33s. a week; that whilst in the building trade wages were 5s. a day of ten hours, in 1877 they were 9d. an hour; and that seamen's wages have risen from 40s. and 55s. a month in 1848, to 70s. and 80s. in 1878. In addition to this increase of wages, Mr. Giffen believes that there has been a considerable shortening of the hours of labour, amounting to 20 per cent. in the textile, engineering, and building trades.

Then as to prices, we find that, whilst wheat averaged 58s. 7d. a quarter between 1837 and 1846, it averaged only 48s. 9d. a quarter between 1876 and 1886. Then in most other things there has been a considerable fall. For example, in 1840 sugar cost 68s. 8d. per cwt.; in 1886 it cost only 21s. 9d. In 1840 cotton cloth cost 5¾d. per yard; in 1886 it cost 3½d. per yard. But the most remarkable results are obtained by comparing the amount of foods consumed per head of the population. Professor Leone Levi finds that in 1820 sugar was consumed to the amount of eighteen pounds per head, and tea to the amount of one pound three ounces; whilst in 1870, of sugar forty-one pounds, and of tea three pounds were consumed per head. Mr. Giffen gives some remarkable figures, and from them we may infer that between the years 1840 and 1881 the consumption per head of bacon and ham has increased thirteen times, of butter six times, of cheese five times, of eggs seven times, of potatoes twelve times, of rice twelve times, of sugar four times, and of wheat five times. It is true that meat has gone up in price, but then meat was during the early part of the century hardly eaten at all by the poor. House rent, too, has increased—according to Mr. Giffen, 150 per cent.; but (putting aside an improvement in the houses in many cases) the increase of rent would not by any means swallow up the gain obtained in other ways.

Looking at the history of wages and prices generally, we may infer that, in the thirteenth century, and during the period which Professor Rogers calls the "golden age," though wages were excessively low, yet this was more than compensated for by the exceeding cheapness of food. Again, there can be no doubt that since that time, until within the last fifty years, the condition of the labouring classes has been wretched in the extreme. In the words of Professor Rogers, the wages of labour have been a bare subsistence, constantly supplemented by the poor-rate. Professor Rogers is of opinion that the condition of the labouring classes during the earlier period compares favourably with their present condition. It is true that food in average years was cheap; but even Professor Rogers admits that in bad years numbers perished from hunger. It avails little that a man can get food for almost nothing one year, if in the next he must starve. Professor Rogers admits, too, that the food was coarse; he might have added that it was sadly wanting in variety. Putting aside such things as tea, coffee, and sugar, there were wanting even such simple things as potatoes and cabbages. But whatever view we may take of these early times, we must be forced to admit that, as regards the amount of wages and their purchasing power, the condition of the labouring classes is now immensely superior to its condition at any time for nearly three hundred years.

NOTE.—Since this essay was written in 1887, a number of Acts have been passed to ameliorate the condition of the working-classes. Moreover, labour questions seem to engage the attention of Parliament in an ever-increasing degree. The question of the hours of labour in particular is becoming very important, and even now sways voters at elections as much as the Home Rule question. It should be observed, too, that the increased working expenses of railway and other companies point to the tendency of the rate of wages to move upwards. Neither does the cost of necessaries bear more hardly than it did. Rather the contrary. The reduction in the duty on tea, for instance, has made that commodity appreciably cheaper.

V.

SOCIALISTIC LEGISLATION IN ANGLO-SAXON COMMUNITIES.

SOCIALISM is a subject which at the present moment is very much in evidence. It is discussed in every review, and debated at the meetings of every religious and scientific association. But it is one of those terms which is apt to be used by different persons in different senses, and to convey different meanings to different minds. It eludes the grasp with a Protean slipperiness. Nothing can be more important, however, in discussions of this sort than to see clearly what socialism means, and to pin it down, so to speak, to one particular sense. The word has, however, been used so differently by writers of authority, that it is difficult to do this. Communism and socialism have been inextricably confused. Nevertheless, the socialism of the present day is generally held to be a socialism only to be realized through the action of the state. Professor Flint defines it to be "the government of all by all and for all, with private property largely or wholly done away, landowners got rid of, capital rendered collective, industrial armies formed under the control of the state on co-operative principles, and work assigned to every individual and its value determined for him." Schäffle, in his "Quintessence of Socialism," says, "Critically, dogmatically and practically, the cardinal thesis stands out—collective instead of private ownership of all instruments of production (land, factories, machines, tools, etc.), 'organization of labour by society,' instead of the distracting competition of private capitalists; that is to say, corporate organization and management of the process of production in the place of private businesses; public organization of the labour of all on the basis of collective ownership of all the working materials of social labour; and, finally, distribution of the collective output of all kinds of manufacture in proportion to the value and amount of the work done by each worker." Mr. Rae, in the *Contemporary Review,* has described it succinctly somewhat in this way. It is, he says, the progressive nationalization of industries with the view to the progressive equalization of incomes. These descriptions give a very clear idea of what is meant, at any rate, by state socialism. But socialism itself is often confounded with what are really only tendencies towards it. The alarm is sometimes raised that socialism is, so to speak, thundering at our gates, whereas there really exists nothing else than a flow or tendency, which would, no doubt, if it burst into a tempestuous flood, carry us into socialism. This tendency is government interference, or legislative interference, or socialistic legislation. Socialism is a system, which would exhibit government interference in the fullest operation. It is the zenith of that state interference which would make the hand of government felt in every hour and every act of the individual's life. Any legislation, therefore, that extends the power of the government to interfere in private life, is rightly called socialistic. It brings us one step nearer to the goal which is the hope and dream of every socialist. Every Act of Parliament that gives the government new interfering powers marks a milestone passed upon the way. It is legislation of this sort which the Liberty and Property Defence League has been formed to combat, and against which Lord Bramwell and Lord Wemyss so stoutly protest.

There can be no doubt, indeed, that in the British Islands the tendency of legislation has been for some years past, and still is, in an increasing degree, in the direction of Government interference. It may be further asserted with some confidence that democracy, in Anglo-Saxon communities at least, the stronger it grows, the more it demands such interference. The more the franchise has been extended in England, the greater has been the demand for interference by the legislature. To demonstrate this would be to go into the history of legislation for the last fifty years or more. But there can be no doubt of the fact, and in order to see how far legislation of this sort is likely to go, it is worth inquiring how far legislation in other countries tends to move in the same direction. An inquiry of this sort will perhaps throw some light upon the question whether legislative interference at home is likely to recede or advance. It is on the whole, perhaps, better to confine our attention to Anglo-Saxon communities. Arguments drawn from foreign nations, where the whole conditions are different, are often misleading. Democracies of the Latin races, for instance, act quite different from Anglo-Saxon democracies. The argument from analogy is not safe where conditions are very different, and the conditions of Anglo-Saxon communities are much more sure to be like those at home than those of foreign races.

The great Anglo-Saxon communities of the world besides the British Islands are the United States of America, and the colonies of Canada and Australia. We will consider the case of the United States first.

The United States demonstrate even more clearly than England that democracies tend more and more to demand legislative interference. And this is the more remarkable because it is one of the fundamental dogmas of the American people that the less of such interference the better. The strength of the tendency of the American democracy to demand legislative interference may be estimated by the fact that in America legislation has gone far beyond the limits theoretically imposed upon it. The practice has prevailed over what is at once philosophic theory and popular maxim.

A brief examination of the facts of American legislation will show this to be so. Professor Bryce, in his "The American Commonwealth," has classified legislative interference under the following heads:—

1. Prohibitions to do acts which are not in the ordinary sense of the word criminal.

K

2. Directions to individuals to do things which it is not obviously wrong to omit.

3. Interferences with the ordinary course of law in order to protect individuals from the consequences of their own acts.

4. Directions to a public authority to undertake work which might be left to individual action, and the operation of supply and demand.

Now, " in every one of these kinds of legislative interference," says Mr. Bryce, "the Americans, or at least the Western States, seem to have gone farther than the British Parliament." It would be difficult to find a case, where the British Parliament has interfered, where the legislature of some American State has not interfered also, and where the latter bodies have interfered, they have generally done so with a heavier and more far-reaching hand. A few illustrations taken from several classes of government interference will suffice to show this. In the first place, the United States are strongly protectionist in policy. They have lately carried protection to an extreme degree by the new tariff provided by the McKinley Act. Protection is really a very gross form of interference with individual liberty, because it is nothing less than compulsion applied to consumers generally to buy at high prices in order to benefit particular manufacturers. This is one broad and general instance, which is common to most other countries besides the United States. Let us consider more particular instances. Under the head of public health, take the case of the manufacture and sale of oleomargarine. The Federal Government has put a heavy tax upon manufacturers of oleomargarine, while the State of Pennsylvania forbids its sale altogether. The State of Georgia compels proprietors of public houses to notify to their guests by public notice or to mention on the bill of fare if oleomargarine is used at their houses. Take, again, the practice of medicine. The State of Illinois has provided that itinerant vendors of any drug or nostrum, and persons publicly professing to cure disease by such means, are to pay a licence of 100 dollars per month. Take, again, the question of the regulation of the liquor traffic. Interference here has gone much further than in England. Some States, as Kansas and North and South Dakota, have prohibited the sale of intoxicating liquor altogether. Others have adopted various forms of local option. Other and more novel provisions are to be found in some States. In the State of Illinois, for instance, liquor-dealers are held responsible for damage done by persons who have become intoxicated on liquor sold by them, and the owner or lessee of the premises is also held responsible if he knowingly allowed such sale to take place. In the State of New York, the sale of liquor to an Indian, minor, or habitual drunkard after notice is given, is illegal, and a similar responsibility to that in the State of Illinois is imposed on the owner or lessee. In the State of Georgia, a person taking out a licence must execute a bond conditioned on keeping an orderly house, and not supplying minors without the consent of parents or guardians.

Turning to another class of cases, we find that banks, insurance companies, benefit societies, and railway companies are more strictly regulated than in England. In many cases the accounts are subject to inspection by government officials, and returns must be made to the government. Then, again, regulations affecting labour are more far-reaching. In England children under ten years of age are not allowed to be employed at all, and those under fourteen years not more than half-time, while minors under eighteen years and women of any age are not to be employed more than ten hours a day. But in Pennsylvania children under thirteen years of age are not allowed to be employed at all, and minors under sixteen years may be employed but nine months in the year, and then only on condition that they attend school during the rest of the year. In the State of New York, children under thirteen years cannot be employed at all. In the State of Georgia, the hours of labour in cotton, woollen, and other manufacturing establishments, and in machine shops, are, for minors under the age of twenty-one years, from sunrise to sunset, with the customary hours for meals, and contracts with parents for such services for a longer time are void. In the State of California, children may not be employed for more than eight hours a day except in agricultural or domestic work. In the States of Pennsylvania and Illinois, eight hours constitutes a day's work when no contract exists to the contrary. There are, however, many exceptions to this. In the State of New York, eight hours constitutes a day's work when no contract exists to the contrary, except in farm or domestic labour, and this provision applies to all mechanics, working men, and labourers employed by

the State or by municipal corporations for the perform-
ance of public works. In the State of California a
similar law prevails. In the State of Texas, it is provided that where a contractor becomes bankrupt, the
labourers employed by him shall have a right of action
against the company or person for whose benefit the
work on which they were employed was done; while
the State of Minnesota enacts that all labour performed
by contract upon a building shall be a first lien thereon.
Some States have succeeded in establishing boards of
arbitration for labour-disputes. Both the States of New
York and Massachusetts provide that the Governor
shall appoint yearly a board of arbitration consisting
of three members. In Massachusetts the board decides
disputes directly, but in New York it only hears ap-
peals from local boards chosen by the disputing parties
and licensed by the county judges.

There are, moreover, many minor points of legislative interference, which, by their curiosity and novelty,
illustrate more pointedly the question under consideration. The following examples have been picked out at
random. The State of New York, for instance, provides that no guest shall be excluded from any hotel
on account of race, creed, or colour. The State of
Georgia orders railway companies to put up a bulletin
stating how much any train already half an hour late
is overdue, while the State of Minnesota prescribes the
character of the waiting-rooms to be provided at
stations. The State of Maryland has instituted a state
Board of Commissioners for practical plumbing, and
licences for plumbers. The State of Texas makes it a

misdemeanour to deal in "futures," or keep a "bucket-shop" for dealing in "futures." The State of Georgia puts a tax of five hundred dollars a year on dealers in "futures," while the State of Ohio punishes any one who offers to sell options, or quotes the prices of "margins," "futures," or "options." The State of New York punishes any one who shall send a letter with intent to cause annoyance to any other person. The State of Nebraska prohibits the sale of tobacco to minors, and the State of Iowa punishes the giving or selling of pistols to them. Both the States of Kentucky and Minnesota have enacted laws which are interesting as embodying provisions somewhat similar to those which have been demanded here with regard to mural advertisements. The State of Kentucky prohibits the sale of any book or periodical, the chief feature of which is to record the commission of crimes, or display by cuts or illustrations of crimes committed, or the pictures of criminals, desperadoes, or fugitives from justice, or of men or women influenced by stimulants. The State of Minnesota similarly prohibits the sale of books and papers devoted to the publication of and principally made up of criminal news, police reports, or accounts of criminal deeds, or pictures and stories of deeds of bloodshed, lust, or crime. Then, again, many states contain provisions against usury, while some create far-reaching exemptions from attachments and executions. Indeed, to such an extent has this been carried that it has been said that the tendency in America is " to require the repayment of debts only when it can be made out of superfluous accumulated capital."

Now, it must be admitted that the tendency towards Government interference at first sight seems irresistibly strong. It may well be thought that, if such things can be done in America, where the people are so energetic and self-reliant, and where it is almost a popular maxim that a man knows his own business best, and should be allowed to do it as he pleases, the prospect of restricting Government interference at home must be faint indeed. But on looking somewhat closer into the matter, it will be found that certain allowances must be made, which somewhat alter the aspect of the matter. It will be found that certain conditions exist in America, which do not exist in this country, and that, in the absence of these conditions, it would be rash to infer that Government interference in England must approximate to such interference in America either in kind or degree. Indeed, it will be found that the opposite is the case. Much as Great Britain and the United States resemble one another, there are well-marked differences between them. Now, one of the great differences is this. In Great Britain the various industries are on the whole tolerably well scattered about in various directions. Manufacturing, mining, and agricultural pursuits are frequently carried on in the same county, and even where a county is devoted to a single industry, this counts for little when counties are, comparatively speaking, so small. But in America it is far otherwise. There are found not merely whole states, but whole groups of states— that is to say, districts vastly larger than England, devoted to particular industries. There are, for instance, the corn-growing states, the cattle-raising states, the mining states, the timber-growing states, and so forth. Now, when we come to examine the statute-books of any state which is the home of any particular industry, we find that it is largely made up of provisions for the protection and encouragement of that particular industry. Take, for instance, the great corn-growing and agricultural State of Minnesota. There we find a great mass of legislation for the protection of farmers. The railways have been forced to make all sorts of concessions to the farming industry, loans of grain seed are granted, agricultural bureaus and fairs are established, lecturers on agriculture are sent round, homesteads are exempted from executions, State Dairy Commissioners are appointed, and the sale and manufacture of oleomargarine narrowly restricted. And so on, *mutatis mutandis* with the other states. So that it is evident that a great deal of Government interference is interference with the object of protecting and encouraging the particular industries that are centred in the several states. This is, no doubt, at best a questionable policy, and it is a selfish and short-sighted policy where it is detrimental to the practice of other industries. But, whatever its merits or demerits, the important thing to remember is that such a policy would be impossible for Great Britain, with its many and diverse interests, with its various industries scattered in all directions. To put Great Britain on similar conditions with many of the American states, we should have to imagine Great Britain a country devoted wholly to one particular industry. We should have to suppose it an entirely agricultural or mining community, just as the State of Minnesota is an agricultural, and the State of Nevada a mining community. But this is very far from being the case. So that clearly the industrial conditions of many of the American states are quite different from those of Great Britain, and one of the causes that impel so many of the American states into legislative interference is found to operate there only by reason of the peculiarity of their conditions, and would be inoperative where the conditions are entirely different. Here, then, is one reason why Government interference is unlikely to go as far in this country as it has done in America, for we have found to be absent here a cause which is there fertile in consequences.

Then, again, another reason why Government interference has gone farther in the American states is to be found in the difference in character between the British Parliament and the average American State Legislature. So long as we have men of the type of the Duke of Argyle and the Earl of Derby in the House of Lords, and Mr. Goschen in the House of Commons, there is not much fear of the British Parliament venturing on legislation like that which is the product of many of the American State Legislatures. Of these latter bodies, Mr. Bryce says that in them the American people "possess bodies with which it is easy to try legislative experiments, since these bodies, though not of themselves disposed to innovation, are mainly composed of men unskilled in economics, inapt to foresee any but the nearest consequences of their measures, prone to gratify any whim of their constituents, and open to the pressure of any section whose self-interest or impatient philanthropy clamours for some departure from the general principles of legislation. For crotchet-mongers as well as for intriguers there is no such paradise as the lobby of a state legislature. No responsible statesman is there to oppose them, no warning voice will be raised by a scientific economist."

It is obvious, from this description of the American State Legislatures, that they differ widely in character from the British House of Commons, and that they are much more prone to plunge into legislative caprices. What kind of legislation they are capable of may be readily inferred from the illustrations which have already been given. What they might be capable of in the future may be gathered from Bills introduced, but which did not become law. Here are two examples from the state of Minnesota. In that State in 1885 a Bill was introduced to prohibit the two sexes from skating at rinks together, and another Bill to license drinkers instead of liquor-sellers! We might almost exclaim with the writer in the Anti-Jacobin—

"Primordial nonsense springs to life
In the wild war of democratic strife."

Sir H. S. Maine has expressed an opinion that the provision of the United States Constitution (Article I. sec. 10), which prohibits any state from passing a law impairing the obligation of any contract, has operated to check socialistic legislation. This, no doubt, has prevented certain legislation of a kind that has appeared on the British statute-books. It would have

rendered impossible the passing of some of the Irish
Land Acts, and certain provisions in the Agricultural
Holdings Acts, which enables a tenant to violate his
contract with his landlord. But probably this part of
the American Constitution has produced very little
effect on the whole. But we may fairly conclude,
however, that legislative interference is unlikely to
go as far in England as it has done in America,
because, as we have seen, the American State Legislatures differ so much from our own, and because, in the
next place, the industrial conditions of many American
states are peculiar, and differ greatly from those of
England.

Turning from the Anglo-Saxon community of the
United States to the British Colonies, in Canada and
Australasia we find that legislative interference has
gone further than at home, as it has done in the
United States. Take the case of Canada first. It is
in the first place protectionist, which, as we have seen,
is really a great piece of Government interference.
Then, again, the state and municipalities largely assist
railways. But it is with regard to the regulations as
to the sale of intoxicants that interference has gone
farthest. In many parts of Canada the sale of intoxicants is forbidden altogether, and in some parts it has
been forbidden, but the restriction has subsequently
been removed. This is as far as interference can
possibly go. It does appear a great interference with
liberty of action to be forbidden to purchase wine,
beer, or spirits. There is Sunday closing nearly everywhere, and in many places it is forbidden to sell liquor

to minors and Indians. In Ontario there is in operation what is known as the Civil Damages Clause in
the United States. It is provided that if a man in
a state of intoxication dies through suicide or some
misadventure, damages may be obtained against the
seller of the liquor by the friends of the deceased.
Then there is a provision in some provinces that no
liquor is to be supplied to any person whose relatives
declare before a magistrate that he is wasting his
means or interfering with the happiness of his family
by drinking. It is clear that these provisions must,
in matters of drinking, tend greatly to restrict individual liberty. The Factory Acts of Canada are not
quite so advanced as in England. In Ontario and
Quebec the Acts are not strictly enforced, because
they are not the same in both provinces, and each
province fears the competition of the other if it puts
its own Act in force. Truck, too, prevails to some
extent in the maritime provinces and Newfoundland.
There is no legal working day, but ten hours is, in
practice, the working day, with many exceptions.
One curious piece of interference should in conclusion
be noticed, and that is, that in Ontario there is some
severe local legislation against Sunday excursions.
This must surely be where the Scotch colonists pre-
dominate. On the whole, therefore, the conclusion
seems to be that Canada has gone further than England
in Government interference.

Turning next to the Australian Colonies and New
Zealand, we meet with a very striking state of things.
Sir Charles Dilke, who can speak with authority, says,

in his "Problems of Greater Britain," that "democracy and state socialism have completely triumphed in Victoria," and further, that "indeed, the strongest disposition exists in Victoria, and, though in a less degree, throughout Australia generally, to think that the state is able to influence the prosperity of a country to a larger extent than is believed possible by us in Great Britain, or by our descendants in Canada or the United States." Professor Playfair once remarked that the activity and perseverance of mankind are continually defeating the folly and caprice of their governors. The Australians, on the contrary, seem to think that the folly and caprice of mankind can be checked or rendered innocuous by the wisdom of the state. At any rate, their domestic policy seems to bear out this view. The colonies are all in the first place, except New South Wales, protectionist. Victoria is so most strongly, and even New South Wales now shows an inclination to recede from free trade. The railways in Australia are everywhere in the hands of the state, but New Zealand now allows them to be built by private enterprise, and gives grants of lands in aid. It must be admitted that the results of the state ownership of railways are admirable. Most of the Australian Colonies assist charities and hospitals, and New South Wales has given work to the unemployed. Most of them, too, assist elementary education and the universities. In Victoria elementary education is free. In New South Wales, South Australia, and Tasmania it is not entirely free, but it is compulsory. In Victoria state aid is given to the

study of botany and astronomy, to schools of mines
and designs. State encouragement is also given to
mining, and to experimental work in horticulture and
agriculture, and prizes are given for fruit and many
other products. In Victoria, too, the state helps to
construct parks, and assists municipalities in making
tramways. Quite lately it has undertaken a great
system of irrigation. Victoria, too, curiously enough,
prohibits the sale of Sunday newspapers. The question of an eight-hours working day has attracted much
attention in Australia, but the law has nowhere yet
interfered to make it compulsory, though it has gone
very near doing so. In the Victorian Parliament, an
abstract proposition in favour of an eight-hours legal
day has been adopted. In Queensland an Eight-Hours
Bill was passed in 1889 by the Lower House, but it
was rejected by the Upper House ; and the very same
thing happened in South Australia. In Victoria, however, an Act was passed in 1885 to make compulsory
early closing in shops. The power of putting the law
in force was left to municipalities, and was at first a
failure ; but public opinion was so strongly in favour
of it that it is now completely successful. In Victoria,
too, eight hours is the working day fixed for labour on
Government works. All the Australian Colonies have
excellent factory laws, and laws directed against sweat-
ing. Whether the anti-Chinese legislation must be
classed as State interference is doubtful, because it
is directed against foreigners. But, on the other hand,
it might well interfere with the liberty of those who
might wish to employ Chinese labour.

Turning our attention to State interference as it affects the liquor trade, we find it to be very vigorous— indeed, almost as much so as in Canada. There is a local option law in force in Queensland; but no compensation is allowed to owners of houses that are closed. In Victoria, on the other hand, compensation is allowed. In South Australia, Tasmania, and New Zealand, a drunkard may be put under notice before a magistrate, in the same manner as we have seen to be the case in Canada. Sunday closing, too, is common.

In New Zealand, the state has undertaken functions which have not yet been undertaken by the state in any other country. The most important of these is the Government Life Insurance. This has been extraordinarily successful in New Zealand, and private insurance offices have been left quite behind. The other is the Public Trust Office, which is also successful; but not so much so as the Life Insurance Office.

It is clear, then, that State interference has been invoked in the Australasian colonies and Canada much more than it has been at home. And it must be admitted that, unless the conditions prevailing there differ widely from those at home, it is probable that English legislation is likely to tend in the same direction. The only well-marked difference is that the colonies are new countries in process of development, and that they are peopled with a race in the full blush and vigour of youthful life. There can be no doubt that legislation may be proper and necessary in a new country, which would be quite unjustifiable in an old one. So that we need not expect all colonial legislation to be acceptable at home. Then, with regard to the character of the colonial legislatures, it is no disparagement to them to say that at present they cannot hope to produce as many capable legislators as the old country. Some of their statesmen would, of course, adorn any assembly; but it is contrary to reason to suppose that a small population can produce as much ripe wisdom as a large one. So that we must expect colonial legislatures to go further than our own House of Commons would think desirable.

There is another good reason for believing that socialistic legislation is not likely to go far in England, or, at all events, that socialism of a revolutionary type will not be embraced, and that is the character of the British working man, a character which no doubt belongs in some degree to the Anglo-Saxon of America, but which is pre-eminently the mark of the working man in our own islands. The character of the Anglo-Saxon in America must have become largely modified by the enormous influx of population from the European continent. But at home it is not so, and there the fact must be at once noted that socialism in any form is utterly alien to the genius of the British working man. He is decidedly πρακτικὸς and hard-headed, and has plenty of what the Greeks called αὐτάρκεια. He is not easily led away by an idea, and possesses that "sullen resistance to innovation," and that "unalterable perseverance in the wisdom of prejudice," that Burke so admired in his countryman. Socialism never has nor ever will take deep root in England. The great socialistic thinkers have been foreigners, like Marx, Lassalle, St. Simon, and Fourier. Socialism in England has never been more than an ephemeral growth. And this is the more remarkable, when it is considered that in no country in the world has the power of capital been so great as in England. It almost seems to challenge by its very bigness the violent opposition of the wage-earning class. Yet the fact remains that it is in this spirit of independence and self-help that the British labouring-classes differ most from those classes on the Continent. This difference has lately been brought out with remarkable force and clearness by Dr. Baernreither, in his important work on "English Associations of Working Men." For it was this difference in character that impressed him more than anything else. In one place he writes, "The free union of individuals for the attainment of a common object is the great psychological fact in the life of this people, its great characteristic feature." Again he writes, "Much that in England can be left to the self-help of the classes concerned, can only be accomplished on the Continent by the more vigorous intervention of the Government. Yet on this very point the study of English institutions should act as an antidote against any exaggerated idea that a Government, by its mere action, can at once remedy every defect. The consideration of working men's relations in England should convince us that State action should merely resemble a prop which supports a building, so long as it is in course of construction, but which is intended to be removed directly the building is compact and complete. The necessity and duty on the

L

Continent of taking care, wherever the action of Government must step in, simultaneously and systematically to awaken and educate self-reliance and spontaneous activity, this is the great lesson which we should derive from the study of English relations." In another place he remarks that the state on the Continent "is continually developing into something outside of and above the nation, entrusted, nay, overburdened with the task of supporting the whole community, and acting as the political and economical guardian of the masses;" and he declares that, while "on the Continent we perceive an enlightened absolutism penetrating deeply all relations of society, in England we see a people who, whether in larger or smaller centres of administration, are essentially self-governing," and, further, that under the Continental system "the spontaneous energies of the people must necessarily be stunted." These statements, coming as they do from such an authority as Dr. Baernreither,* carry great weight with them. They are in the highest degree significant, and pregnant with suggestion, and throw a strong light on the character of the British working-classes, their independence, self-help, and associative spirit. A French writer, M. Julian Decraix, has lately remarked on the same thing in an article in the *Revue des Deux Mondes*. In a description of Liverpool, he is led to dwell on "the advantages of private initiative, in an age in which it has become

---

* This work by Dr. Baernreither has been translated into English, and contains a very appreciative preface by Mr. Ludlow, the chief registrar of friendly societies.

the fashion to call at every moment upon the State for intervention, which is generally useless." The English working-classes have, indeed, already become in a large measure their own insurers, through the agency of the different classes of friendly and provident societies, their own protectors in trade disputes by means of trades unions, and to some extent, capitalists by means of co-operative societies. In these departments they have greatly surpassed their fellows on the Continent. In Germany quite recently a great scheme of insurance for sick, aged, and infirm workmen has had to be undertaken. Unlike the Frenchmen or the Germans, they do not keep importuning with useless prayer the legislative idol, nor do they give point to the saying of Polybius, that men, though apparently the wisest of animals, are really the silliest, because they persistently have recourse to devices which have often failed them before. This very spirit of independence, however, tends to bring trouble with it. No one can commend what is called the new trades unionism, with its new-fangled theories, and utter disregard of the different conditions that prevail in the various fields of labour. No one, again, can do anything but condemn the violence shown towards non-unionists, or the inefficiency of the work, which shipowners say exists at the London Docks.

The working-classes of Canada and Australia must be credited with quite as much self-reliance and power of self-help as their kinsmen at home. Friendly societies and trades unions flourish there exceedingly well. Co-operative societies, however, have not taken

much root, partly, no doubt, owing to the prosperity
of the colonists, which makes them indifferent to the
small savings to be gained by co-operative distribution.
Much as they are inclined to call for State intervention
they have not forgotten the value of self-reliance.
Nothing, indeed, can be farther from the mind of the
colonists than extreme socialistic ideas. Extreme
views on the land question, however, have been held
by colonial political leaders. Nationalization of the
land, which was promulgated as a theory in Victoria
long before it was taken up by Mr. Henry George,
is advocated by some, but it makes no way amongst
the people.

Then, again, there is one element in much of the
Government interference as developed in England and
the colonies, and particularly in America, which to
some extent renders that interference less objectionable
than it otherwise would be. This element is the
endeavour to make law and morality more nearly coincident in their spheres. This endeavour is, at least,
healthy, though it may, and sometimes does, go beyond
what expediency allows. Examples of this sort of
interference are common enough in America. Such
are the laws of the States of Texas, Georgia, and Ohio,
which are aimed at gambling in stocks and shares, and
that of the State of New York, which punishes any
person who shall send a letter with intent to cause
annoyance to any other person. In England, too, an
Act has lately been passed by Parliament, the object of
which is to check misrepresentations by promoters and
directors of companies. It is, of course, a mere truism

to say that men cannot be made moral by Act of Parliament. But in so far as they indicate a determination on the part of the community that men shall be punished for doing what right conscience condemns, such laws are absolutely good. They at least show a healthy feeling to be prevalent in society, and they demonstrate to a possible wrong-doer that public opinion is against him, and that is an opinion which he shrinks from outraging. It is only when law goes so far in advance of practical morality, that it can only be enforced with difficulty or not at all, that the tendency to make law and morals coincident becomes mischievous. This element in Government interference is, then, as far as it goes, a good one, and it makes Government interference wear a less sinister aspect than it otherwise would do. There is one other element in Government interference, which is near akin to what may be called the moral element, and of which much the same may be said. This is what may be justly termed the philanthropic element. A very considerable portion of legislative interference is really due to feelings of philanthropy. Men see much suffering about them, and they grow impatient at the sight. They are unwilling to let natural causes painfully and slowly work out what is probably the only remedy. Their feelings are outraged by the notion of "the struggle for existence," and "the survival of the fittest," operating as causes without restraint in human society. All this is good in itself, and philanthropy only becomes bad when, in a fit of irrational impatience, it adopts a remedy which may be worse than the disease. Moreover, attempts to invoke the aid of the Government to cure the evils that prevail in society are useful in two ways. They pointedly call attention to evils that might otherwise pass unnoticed by the great mass of society, and they sometimes indicate the direction in which the remedy must be sought; and in so far as they do this, they are far from being useless. And when it is considered that it is the end of all legislation to promote human happiness, it will be at once seen that any step that tends to further this end in any degree, however small, is not without its value.

It should be remembered, too, that legislation has interfered with individual freedom upon all sorts of grounds, political, moral, and religious, and such interference has been considered natural, and no one ever associated them with socialistic tendencies. Sunday trading has been forbidden on religious grounds, yet it is a gross interference with the liberty of the atheist. It is not permitted to use dogs for drawing light carts, because it is considered cruel. Tobacco can only be grown under stringent regulations. Posts and telegraphs are made a State monopoly. These are a few instances of the many ways in which the State interferes to limit freedom. A man is restricted in all sorts of ways, purely on grounds of general convenience. What the difference in principle is between many legal restrictions which are considered reasonable and proper, and some of the modern legislative acts, which are condemned as socialistic, it is difficult to see. Legislation within the present century has increased by leaps and bounds, because it is more and more believed that wherever law can ameliorate the conditions of life, it may be rightly invoked. This is the working theory, if it may be so called, of practical legislation, and though it may have a socialistic tendency in restricting liberty, it certainly is not socialistic in aim.

Lastly, the feeling of objection that is shown against Government interference arises in a great measure from a radical misconception of the nature of the democratic system of government. So long as government is in the hands of a few, the great majority of the people having no part therein, then indeed the governors and the governed stand apart; and when the governed clamour for some sort of legislative interference, they are asking for something from a class standing apart from and above themselves. But in a democracy it is far otherwise. Then the governing body is really the servant or agent of the people, and when the people demand Government interference, they are no longer in the position of suppliants to a superior body, but rather in that of masters commanding a servant, or principals an agent. Government interference looked at from this point of view wears a very different aspect. For when it comes from a superior and separate body in answer to the demands of the people, it is something in the nature of a favour granted; it is, so to speak, the extended hand of protection, and merits the epithet "paternal." But such interference, when it comes from a body popularly elected by a majority, is in no sense "paternal," for it really comes from the people themselves. A whole people cannot any more than an individual exercise a "paternal" government over itself. And this consideration really removes much of the ground of objection to Government interference. It is continually said that such interference is "paternal," is "grandmotherly," and saps the spirit of self-help and self-reliance. But where the Government is popular, it is difficult to see how this can be so.

It has been already suggested that Government interference tends to grow with the advance of democracy. Now, why this should be so becomes clear when the true nature of democracy is considered. Professor Bryce puts it very well, when he says, "And in some countries, of which England may be taken as the type, the transference of political power from the few to the many has made the many less jealous of Government authority. The Government is now their creature, their instrument—why should they fear to use it? They may strip it to-morrow of the power with which they have clothed it to-day. They may rest confident that its power will not be used contrary to the wishes of the majority among themselves." Why indeed, one may well ask, should they hesitate to use the instrument, to obtain which whole nations have suffered the bitter pangs of revolution? .

And in this way, a democratic form of government may resemble a "paternal" form of government. But it will be a resemblance merely, for the two are in reality very different, though the results may appear much the same. So that Government interference in

·democracy may not be so objectionable as is often supposed. For if the majority think fit to apply the sanctions of the law to enforce the carrying out of that which they already approve, why should they not do so? It is really only a wider application of what is done every day by a trades union, or some other body where the majority impose their will. If it is not objectionable that a trades union should restrict the hours of labour for its members to eight hours a day, why should it be objectionable that a majority in the state should restrict the hours of labour to eight hours for all labourers whatever? It cannot be objected that legislative interference would tend to protect the interests of some at the expense of others, because the legislative interference is invoked in the interests of the majority; and it is part of the theory of democratic government that the majority must prevail, but that the minority must give way.·

For the reasons, then, which have been indicated, it is unlikely that socialistic legislation will go as far in England as it has done in America and the colonies. For the conditions which are there favourable to its growth are here largely absent. That the law will be ·called in aid more and more to ameliorate life is, however, very probable. That legislation will sometimes fail in its objects, or even prove mischievous, is also in some degree probable. But even legislative failures, injurious as they are, may be forgiven. For legislative interference is often at least healthy in origin. It tends to widen the sphere of morals, and unlock the fountains of philanthropy. Moreover,

when looked at from the point of view of the theory,
that underlies the rule of the people, it seems to harmonize with and to be the complement of that theory.
It may be that sometimes the majority may err in
the means they adopt to gain an end right in itself,
and interference based on wrong methods must of
course be bad. We can then only say with Cicero,
" Male judicavit populus, sed judicavit." But the sort
of legislation that is likely to be adopted in England,
though it may be rightly called socialistic, is a very
different thing from revolutionary socialism. That,
indeed, is about the last thing likely to find favour
in England. On the continent of Europe it may well
be otherwise, because it is customary there to look
more upon Government as a sort of deity. It is a
Pandora with a box full of gifts for men, and, if that
box can be opened, all will be well. In England, on
the other hand, Government is rather looked upon as
an instrument which, if carefully used, may sometimes
be employed with advantage. This difference in the
conceptions of Government is at the root of much
divergence in legislation. The laws of a country may,
indeed, be called its physical expression, like the
features and movements on the human face. They
tell us something of the character of the people. And
just as the laws of England show the love of its people
for individual liberty, so the character of the people
proves that they will tolerate no law that will deprive
them of that liberty.

VI.

SCIENCE AND POLITICS.

It is a commonplace remark that scientific discoveries, and their practical application to the wants of every-day life, make the present century more remarkable for material and utilitarian progress than any that have preceded it within human memory. Other periods of history have been marked by the rise or fall of empires, great revolutions in political institutions, discoveries of unknown continents mysterious with destinies as yet unrevealed, or by a vigorous awakening of art and literature. But when we ask ourselves what it is that in the nineteenth century has most affected human affairs, we at once think of such things as the railway, the steamship, and the electric telegraph. They affect different minds in different ways. To the young, who have been brought up in the midst of them, and to the careless and indifferent, they are hardly more than objects of wonderment, if indeed that. In their minds the express train, and the fast steamers that knit together the outlying parts of great empires, and the globe-girdling wire that flashes its messages from continent to continent, the telephone, and the like, excite at best only a bewildering amazement, but strike no deeper note. Their very familiarity breeds, not indeed contempt, but apathy and indifference. To the man of science and the engineer they are fraught with vast interest. They at once testify to the great wealth of fruit already garnered in by past labourers in the field of science, and are rich with promise for the future. They teem with problems as yet unsolved, and with unknown possibilities for future discovery and improvement. In many ways they present ample food for reflection to the mind of the man of science. To the political philosopher and the statesman they have an interest of a kind different indeed, but no less profound. To their minds they are full of pregnant suggestion. While the physicist is thinking of heat-expansion, the mechanical equivalent of heat, conservation and transmutation of energy, and other kindred subjects, the political inquirer is impelled to think of the effect of these scientific discoveries upon, and their practical application to, forms of government, federation, the size and growth of states, and other human institutions. Professor Freeman has put forward a doctrine, which he says may seem a paradox. He says "that the great practical discoveries of modern science, the use of steam, electricity, any other natural powers, in the various forms in which we have ˉlearned to apply them, are above all things valuable for their political results." A paradox indeed it may at first appear. But when it is remembered that man is, as Aristotle said, a political animal, and that his political relations are, excepting only his religion, the most important thing that concern him, the seeming paradox will vanish. Religion deals with a man's relations to God; politics deal with his relations to his fellow-men. And as the main part of life is concerned with our relations to others, it is clear that scientific discoveries, like literature and the arts, are in truth only important as they affect those relations. The hermit may indeed contemn them, but then, he is only in the world, and not of it; he communes with God, and not with man. But for the remainder of mankind all that affects human intercourse, all that affects political life in the broadest sense, must of necessity be of great concern. It will be, therefore, useful to see in what manner, and to what extent, scientific discovery and material progress influence politics and society.

In the first place, it is worth noting the influence of improved means of travel and communication upon the size, stability, and growth of states. One of the lessons of history is that in the earlier ages of mankind states were often small, sometimes very small indeed, and that when they were large, such states were eminently unstable and liable to decay. The most important examples of small states are of course derived from the history of ancient Greece. This is one of the most striking things that present themselves to the students of Herodotus and Thucydides. In reading their pages, he becomes aware that the Greek state was little more than a city. The Greek politician was, as the word " politician " implies, strictly

one who concerned himself with the affairs of his city.
So, too, it was with Rome for many years. The Roman
state for long remained conterminous with the Roman
city, and it was only by a process of very gradual
expansion that the city became the centre of a widely
extended empire. On the other hand, empires of wide
area almost always contained within themselves the
seeds of dissolution, and were usually transient. The
empire of Alexander the Great is an instance in point.
When deprived of the guidance of his masterful hand,
it fell to pieces at once. It faded like an "insub-
stantial pageant," leaving "not a rack behind." The
Persian Empire is another instance. It is curious
what devices the kings of Persia had to resort to, in
order to keep together their territory, which, compared
with some modern states, was not very large. The
outlying portions of the empire had to be entrusted
by the central government to provincial governors or
satraps. The satraps were an everlasting source of
anxiety. Far removed from the control of the home
government, and the jealous eye of the king himself,
they were apt to arrogate to themselves positions of
semi-independence, and sometimes aspired to carve out
for themselves kingdoms from the territory of their
royal master. In order to check such lofty pretensions, all sorts of ingenious devices were adopted. The
satrap was entrusted with civil powers only, military
authority being placed in other hands. He was
induced, if possible, to espouse a daughter or some
near relative of the king, in order to win his allegiance
to the royal house. And so, by devices of this sort

the Persian monarchs were tolerably successful in preventing rebellion and keeping their heritage intact. Rome, again, affords us an example of the difficulty of maintaining the great empires of antiquity. As in the case of Persia, the government of the provinces had to be entrusted to governors. They took advantage of the absence of central control to rule with a high hand, and to extort and oppress, when they did not rebel. But it was in the time of the Emperors that this absence of control was most fruitful in its results. Then, indeed, legions in the provinces actually proceeded to change dynasties, and to impose some successful general as Emperor upon the helpless citizens at the capital. Otho, Galba, Vitellius, and Vespasian alike owed the imperial purple to the allegiance of the provincial soldiers. In a memorable passage the historian Tacitus relates that on one occasion two common soldiers undertook to transfer the crown, and that they succeeded in their undertaking. The Roman emperors were continually apprehensive of the conduct of their provincial governors. Domitian, for instance, recalled Agricola from Britain, though he was perhaps the most successful commander and explorer of his time, and probably most unjustly suspected. It rarely happened that the relations of the emperor with his governors were as friendly and intimate as the relations between Trajan and the younger Pliny. And finally the great Roman Empire broke up entirely, and Rome herself became, as Byron calls her, "the Niobe of Nations." And in comparatively modern times the tendency for widely extended empires to fall to pieces is still noticeable. The empire of Charles the Fifth, in its full integrity, was not of long duration. France, Holland, Spain, and Portugal have all tried to extend their territory by acquiring colonial possessions, but they have all lost most of what they gained.

It may be said, then, generally that, until quite recently, the successful states of the world have been the small ones, and not the large ones. It is the small ones that have most influenced the destinies of mankind. Athens, Judæa, the Italian republics, the Netherlands, and the British Islands were all small, but they have made a great mark in the world. Rome may appear an exception, but Rome too had more of the essential parts of greatness before it reached its greatest area. When largest in size it was least in soul. But the great states have had comparatively small influence. They have not been able even to sustain themselves. China indeed has for centuries maintained a huge empire. But as far as influence on the world is concerned, it might just as well have been situated in one of the fixed stars. But the last hundred years has seen a reversal of what seemed to be a universal law. States have begun to grow enormously, and they seem destined to retain their bigness. The British Empire is a great example of this. The United States and Russia, again, are also both examples of vast areas subject to a single power. The United States may by this time have reached its ultimate dimensions, but it has grown enormously by such additions as Florida, Louisiana, Texas, and Alaska.

Russia steadily receives accretions in Central Asia, and looks patiently towards an increase of territory in South-Eastern Europe. Though she never hastes, she never rests. It is impossible to believe that she has yet reached her full limits. There is also a correlative tendency to sink small states in large ones. The Grand Duchies of Tuscany and Parma, the Papal States, the kingdom of the Two Sicilies, have all been merged in the kingdom of Italy. The petty German States have been merged in the German Empire. Poland has been effaced from the map of Europe. The present century is marked by two streams running side by side in international politics. The one stream tends to suppress and merge small states, the other to create and consolidate large ones. This is to some extent due, no doubt, to the desire to make races and states coincident. But even to this some limit must be put, as Signor Crispi has had to forcibly remind the Irredendists of Italy. But however that may be, the old order of things is reversed. The future of the world is with the great states, the world-empires, as Professor Seeley calls them. The British Empire, the United States, Russia, and probably China, are the powers of the future. The days of small states, of even moderately large states, are past. Of this the European countries are fully aware, and hence the feverish avarice of the scramble for Africa. M. Prevost Paradol, in his " La France Nouvelle," gave the French an emphatic warning, and strenuously insisted on the French acquisition of a great territory in Northern Africa. It was not out of caprice that M.

Jules Ferry sent expeditions to Tonquin and Mada-
gascar. Neither is it caprice that has sent the Germans
and Italians to East Africa. It was plain to French,
German, and Italian statesmen that, without acquisition
of fresh territory, their countries were doomed to a
future of petty insignificance, which was not a thing
they could complacently dwell upon. Whether even
now these countries will ultimately succeed is doubtful, but they are at least alive to the fact that they
cannot merely stand and mark time, but that they
must either expand or prepare to retire gracefully from
the rank of the great Powers.

Here, then, is a great reversal, a great revolution in
human affairs. And the cause of it is not far to seek.
It is scientific discovery and its practical application.
It is the railway, the steamship, and the telegraph.
The want of means of rapid communication between
the different parts of wide empires was the real cause
of the facility with which in earlier times these
empires fell to pieces. It was all but impossible for
a central government to keep an efficient control over
far distant lands. All manner of untoward events
might take place there before the home authorities
could become aware of them, much less prevent them.
It was little use for a Persian king or Roman emperor
to sit in Susa or on the Palatine concocting administrative measures, promulgating edicts or fulminating
denunciations, when in the far distance his satrap or
proconsul, acting on the proverb, "procul a Jove, procul a fulmine," was either setting his authority at
defiance or sapping his power. Their commands or

rebukes were often hardly more efficacious than a Pope's sentence of excommunication on a British Prime Minister would be. But all this is changed now. Where the railway and the steamship are, there space is practically in part annihilated. A man now can go from London to Canada in about the same time it used to take him to go from London to Edinburgh, and he can reach the Antipodes in a shorter time than he once required for crossing the Atlantic. Even so short a time ago as the time of the American civil war, it took forty days for the British Cabinet to receive an answer to their ultimatum to the United States on the Slidell and Mason incident. It is obvious, therefore, that it is possible to bring the distant parts of a great empire practically into close contiguity with one another. They become one great neighbourhood, and the whole can be kept well under the control of the central government. The telegraph, too, is of immense importance. A colonial governor has not any longer to wait for weeks or months before he can receive instructions from home. They are flashed out to him almost in a moment of time. And, conversely, his acts are instantly made known at home, and are usually made objects of common knowledge through the disseminating power of the press. It is not too much to say that had a fleet of swift steamers been sailing between Liverpool and New York in 1776, the Declaration of Independence might perhaps never have been signed. But when it took weeks to cross the ocean, the British colonies in North America were practically much further away than they are now. The delay

that occurred over the interchange of views between
the home and colonial authorities led to all sorts of
misunderstandings, and events that were in their in-
ception small, by lapse of time became gigantic evils.
It was difficult for both sides to come to any accord.
And not only was the distance then practically greater,
but this distance affected the imagination. It seemed
natural that two countries so far apart should be independent of one another. Nay, it seemed unnatural
that they should be yoked together. Why, it was
argued by the colonists, unite in irritating bonds countries that the hand of nature has placed apart? Why
place together what God has put asunder? But at the
present day it is quite otherwise. Now that far distant countries are brought within easy distance of one
another, it does not seem unnatural that they should
be united. On the contrary, it is usually thought that
such a union would be mutually advantageous. And
surely with reason the same causes may be ascribed to
the failure of France, Holland, Spain, and Portugal, to
keep their important colonies. It has been fortunate
for England that she was able to keep so many of her
colonies in hand, until the introduction of the steamship and the telegraph. As it was, she lost the
United States, and had these scientific discoveries been
longer delayed, she might by this time have lost many
other of her colonial possessions. Thanks, however,
to the practical application of scientific discovery,
the British Empire ranks amongst the first in the
world.

Closely connected with this topic is the influence of

scientific discovery upon decentralization and local government. The difficulties that were formerly encountered in making provincial governments adequate and safe have already been referred to. Owing to the lack of home supervision, such governments were either timidly constructed and therefore feeble, or else entrusted with wide powers which were often abused. But in modern times it is possible to decentralize, and that with impunity, owing to the vastly improved means of communication. Decentralization is a process continually going on. Most of our colonies are now entrusted with parliamentary institutions, and are hardly at all interfered with by the home government. Quite recently Western Australia has been made a self-governing colony. And within the British Islands decentralization still goes on. The railway has brought all parts of the country so near together that this can now be done with ease and safety. In 1888 an important Local Government Act was passed for the counties of England, and in 1889 one was passed for Scotland. And a great party are anxious to bestow a large measure of self-government upon Ireland. Whether it will ever be obtained or not is for the present uncertain. But if it is ever obtained, it will be because rapid means of communication will have rendered it safe to grant it.

The relation borne to federation by scientific discovery is of great importance. Much has been said in a previous essay upon federations generally, so it must be enough here to note the great development of federal institutions within the present century. It is a most remarkable thing that this great development is contemporaneous with the great practical scientific discoveries. There is surely something here more than mere chance. Then further it is noteworthy that just as large states have supplanted small states, so large federations have supplanted small ones. The Achæan League, the United Netherlands and Switzerland, are pigmies when compared with the giants of the United States, Canada, the Argentine Republic, and the coming Australian Federation. Switzerland is, indeed, now the only small federation. She is a sort of survival of the past, and may be placed in the museum of political curiosities, and catalogued as the dwarf confederation. When it is considered that a federal government is at bottom a compromise between the conflicting interests of different portions of territory, in order to meet common dangers and necessities, it becomes clear that it is for the most part likely to be adopted over wide areas. For it is over wide areas that conflicting interests are most likely to arise. But without good means of communication such a union of distant territories would be difficult, if not impossible. There can be little doubt that the great network of railways now spread throughout the United States has made the American Federation infinitely easier than it otherwise would have been. There is always, in such countries as the United States, a danger of a dissolution of their constituent parts. It is impossible to think of the history of the United States without seeing that this is so. The great American civil war will stand as an example and a warning for all time.

But with the lapse of time and the growth of the railway system, the tendency to dissolution tends more and more to a vanishing-point. Never were the United States more united than they are to-day. It is not long since they celebrated the centenary of the inauguration of their first President, and so much enthusiasm was shown in all parts of the great republic that it may now be said with some confidence that it has an assured and well-consolidated unity. This beneficent result must surely be ascribed in a large degree to the railways and the telegraphs. The various states have been brought so near together that their interests are more bound in unison, and are more nearly identical. They are becoming more and more necessary to one another's welfare, and the closer they unite the more advantageous the union becomes. It is the avowed object of the new Tariff Act to make the United States one great neighbourhood, self-sufficing and independent of foreign imports. Bret Harte, in one of his poems, relates what two locomotive engines are fancifully supposed to have said on meeting face to face at the opening of the Union Pacific Railway, after travelling from the Atlantic and Pacific seaboards respectively. But though they are made to boast of much, yet they pass over in silence the greatest boast of all. They might have boasted how they were rendering the Federal Constitution more and more stable. They might have boasted on the fact that they were cementing the union in indissoluble bonds, relegating the horrors of civil war to a dark and nearly forgotten limbo, and assuring in the future a lengthened prospect of peace, founded on neighbourly good-will and identity of interests.

The influence of railways on the neighbouring confederation of the Dominion of Canada is remarkable. Upon no country have railways had so beneficent effect as upon Canada. For a long time it seemed as though Canada, or at least parts of it, were destined to absorption into the United States. Before the introduction of railways, the Canadian north-west provinces were so distant from the eastern provinces that they practically had no connection with one another. Winnipeg was much more closely connected with St. Paul and Minneapolis than with Montreal and Quebec. British Columbia was much more in communication with California and Oregon than with eastern Canada. Emigration in Canada flowed, not westward, but into New England and New York. But the introduction of railways, particularly the Canadian Pacific Railway, has altered all this. For the future Vancouver will be as closely connected with Quebec as San Francisco with New York, and the Canadian emigrant will press forward to develop the riches of the north-west instead of crossing over to the already crowded states of New England. And, with regard to Australasian federation, it should here be noticed that it is distance, and distance only, which even fast steamers cannot sufficiently abridge, that keeps New Zealand from coming into a federal union with the Australian colonies.

The relation of scientific discovery to democracy is a subject that is full of interest. Rousseau did not hesitate to declare his opinion that democracy was

incompatible with a large state. He considered that
the great states of his time were far too big in area,
and he wished for a return to the model of the old
Greek city. What he would have said to the present
British Empire or to the United States it is impossible
to say. But if he were alive now, he would have to
retract his opinion that democracy can only live in a
small state. Montesquieu too seems to have thought
the same thing, but he had the foresight to see that
the difficulty might be got over by federation. And
here again it is from the means of communication that
we have to note the most important consequences. It
will become apparent on reflection that, where communication is difficult and the area large, the democratic form of government is by its very nature not
easy of application. For what does democracy con-
note? Government by the people, or participation
by all in governing. But where distances are great
and communication difficult, the obstacles to the participation of all in governing become immensely
augmented. And so democracies first arose in small
states, and we have to go to the small Greek cities
for the first examples of this form of government. In
the large states like Persia, Assyria, Egypt, we find
that the monarchical form of government existed,
varying in different degrees from a mild paternal rule
to an oppressive and dark despotism. But it was in
the small Greek cities that democracy flourished, for
there it was possible for each citizen to come to the
Assembly and listen to the wild harangues of a Cleon
or the flowing eloquence of a Demosthenes, and to

signify his pleasure as to the policy for his country to adopt. The citizens and the actual administrators of government lived in close propinquity to one another. It is almost as though the whole body of electors to the British House of Commons lived beneath the shadow of Westminster Hall. So that for small states democracy was natural and easy of adoption, and we can understand that it was no wild statement of Pericles when he said that the Athenians accounted a man useless who took no part in public affairs. But in the large states democracy was impossible according to the then known political methods, for representation was a device not then discovered.

One of the most curious and interesting spectacles in ancient history is the difficulty that Rome met with in the later republican period in adjusting her political institutions, which were becoming less and less oligarchical, and beginning to assume a democratic appearance through the widening of the franchise of Roman citizenship. This privilege, which was originally confined to the dwellers on the Seven Hills and the immediate neighbourhood, was gradually extended over the Italian peninsula, and finally much further than this. But how to enable the Roman citizen to exercise his powers as a citizen, and so become a factor in the wheels of government at Rome, was a problem that vexed in vain the minds of her most acute statesmen. The possibility of some means of representation either did not occur to them, or, if it did, they did not see their way to putting it into practice. It is only in comparatively modern times that representation has been introduced. It is an almost necessary incident' of parliamentary government, but until quite recently representation even in small states has been carried out so timidly, and on so limited a scale, that it has been rather oligarchical than democratic in its nature. Until the great Reform Act the British Government was largely aristocratic in character, and certainly oligarchical. But within a period almost coincident with the introduction of a great railway system, it has become democratic. Is this merely a fortuitous circumstance? Surely not. Representation has become easier in consequence of a greatly improved means of communication. The influence of railways on democracy and representative government can hardly be over-estimated. Not that even representation is a full equivalent for a democracy in which every citizen can personally take part. Parliaments do not always faithfully represent the views of the people. Moreover, where areas are large, representation becomes correspondingly difficult. It is no light matter for a Member of Congress to travel from San Francisco or New Orleans to Washington. It would be quite impossible for a member of a British Imperial Parliament to attend from New Zealand or Australia. Representative government in any case has only become possible on any great scale since the discovery of rapid means of communication, and it is for this reason that the wonderful impulse given to democratic.institutions has accompanied the no less wonderful application of science to the conveniences of life, which is the special glory of the present century. It is clear that democracy was at first only possible in small communities, but, thanks to scientific discovery, representation has been made easy. There is now practically no limit to the area over which the democratic form of government can be successfully applied. The most remarkable instance is the United States. That a people numbering over fifty millions, and scattered over an area of about three million square miles, should be subject to one of the most popular governments in the world is surely an amazing fact, and one worth thinking over. There are few more dramatic incidents in modern affairs than the casting of votes over this vast area by this great people for the election of their President, and that too in a single day. It should not be forgotten, too, that the telegraph and the press have in a degree contributed their influence to make representation easy. Representatives are now subjected to the glare of " the fierce light " of popular gaze, and cannot escape the vigilant criticism of their constituents. The people place the more trust in the representative system, because, knowing as they do, their representatives' every word and act, they are well aware that they have them well in hand. In a word, as Professor Freeman says, the great practical discoveries of modern science have " enabled large states to rise to the political level of small ones." These words are a seeming paradox, but they are profoundly true. It has not been until quite recently that any but small states were capable of sustaining democratic institutions. Large states could not come up to their political level. Now they can do so, for scientific discovery has rendered democracy on a great scale possible. And to have done this is as great an achievement as any that the world has yet seen.

And just as democracy has become more possible, so in a corresponding degree has the tyranny either of a despot or an oligarchy become less possible, putting aside those oriental countries as yet untouched by European influences. The easy methods of travel, and the conveniences afforded by the railway, the post-office, the telegraph, and the newspaper, for the transmission and distribution of information, have made tyranny increasingly difficult. Personal inaccessibility and secrecy have always been, and probably still are, necessary for successful tyranny. Surely the notion of "the divinity that doth hedge a king" must have arisen at least in some degree from a certain awe begotten by the withdrawal of the monarch from popular gaze. It was essential that the populace should have little opportunity of witnessing the human frailties of their ruler, or of getting that familiarity that breeds contempt. The story of the Pseudo-Smerdis who succeeded in winning for himself the Persian crown, on the false pretence of royal descent, is full of suggestive meaning. He carried the habit of secrecy to an almost incredible extent. But then it was essential to the maintenance of his position. He kept himself closely confined to his citadel, and his very appearance was unknown to those about the court. His features were as little known as those of the man with the iron mask. Unluckily for him, his personal aspect one day became divulged by an artful contrivance on the part of those who suspected a fraud, and there was soon an end of this adventurer's career as a king. Again, there is a certain grim darkness and mysterious secrecy that seems to shroud the life of the Roman Emperor Tiberius, in the island of Capreæ. And when we read of Philip the Second of Spain, sitting in the Escorial at Madrid, weaving the web of destiny, penning prolix and wearisome despatches with an untiring industry, constant only in duplicity, and hurrying to early and mysterious graves a Montigny or an Escovedo, it is impossible to avoid a shudder at the inscrutable gloom that enshrouded him, which a lapse of three centuries has not entirely dispelled. It may be safely asserted that the march of western civilization has become too rapid to allow the recurrence of such incidents in human affairs as these, unless, indeed, some step of retrogression is reserved for us. For the present, at any rate, we may be sure that there is little chance of secrecy, hardly of privacy even, reserved for those uneasy heads that wear the crown. And if there is little chance for the tyranny of a single man, there is much less for that of a group of men. The insidious workings of a Venetian oligarchy are vanished, let us hope, for ever. When the railway makes travelling easy for all, and when the telegraph and the newspaper bring information to all who can read, nothing at least that is at all likely to shock popular feeling, or outrage humanity, can be for a moment veiled from popular view. Science is indeed the twin brother of Liberty.

, The bearing of scientific discovery on the conduct

of war and prospects of peace is noteworthy. Perhaps the most interesting aspect of this question is the relation of warfare, as modified by our modern inventions, to the comparative sizes of states and forms of government. In the first place, it must be remarked that war has become enormously costly, and. is likely to become more and more so in an increasing degree. The military and naval budgets of Continental nations, even in times of peace, have reached appalling dimensions. Almost every year sees some addition to them. The cost of a first-class ship of war and its guns may well disquiet the mind of the poor tax-payer. No European country can afford to be without such weapons of offence as torpedoes, colossal guns, and rifles and swords of the newest and most efficient type. But this security is gained at an enormous cost. No wonder that Europeans are beginning to think that their countries are being "run" for the advantage of America. It seems, therefore, a natural consequence that the richest countries are likely to be the most successful in war. Of course this need not necessarily be the case, because a nation may be rich and yet too devoted to the pursuits of peace to give the necessary attention to external defence. Riches can never quite compensate for unpreparedness. France was richer than Prussia, but, as it turned out, quite unprepared. And Sir Charles Dilke has expressed his opinion most emphatically on the unpreparedness of Great Britain to meet a sudden attack. In such an event our riches would only form a great prize to our conquerors. And, again, it seems to follow that the largest countries, in so far as mere greatness of extent brings them wealth, would be the most successful. But here, again, it is obvious that a wilderness however extensive, or fertile acres however many, if left untilled, cannot profit at all. So that a small state, if rich, could cope on equal or superior terms with a poor but vastly larger state. However that may be, it is certain that mere hardihood, endurance, and courage cannot count for as much as they once did. They are valuable still, no doubt, but no amount of courage can stand up against the raking fire of a machine-gun. The Mahdists in the Soudan campaign fought with unsurpassable bravery, but they were cut down like grass. The people who bring into the field the most efficient weapons must win, if they handle them with the necessary skill. The Dutch peasantry in the sixteenth century would sometimes arm themselves with all kinds of impromptu weapons, and would give a good account of themselves against the trained battalions from Spain. But it would be little use for any people to attempt any such daring in these days against the soldiers of a modern state. It would be little use for an Alva or Don John of Austria, with all their skill and intrepidity, to direct insufficiently armed troops against a German battalion. No Drake or Howard could have any chance of success, if he relied on mere daring, in the face of a first-class man-of-war. So that it seems almost certain that the richest country has, if it chooses to take advantage of its wealth, the best chance of success in war under its modern conditions. How far, and in what manner, the relations of the different forms of government to war are affected by modern inventions is a different and more complex question. One thing, however, seems certain, and that is that tyranny is not likely to derive much advantage from the increased costliness of war. It would be strange indeed if a tyrant should be rich enough to supply these costly inventions out of his own private purse for use against his subjects for purposes of oppression. And he could hardly expect to derive the necessary money from his subjects by a process of taxation. In former times a tyrant could grind down his subjects by means of a body of troops, small, but attached to his person by self-interest. But that he could hardly do now, at any rate for any length of time. On the other hand, parliamentary government, and the newspapers together, are inimical to successful war. Secrecy from the enemy is one of the elements of success, but at a time and in a country where every item of news is bandied about from mouth to mouth, secrecy, even on the most vital points, is all but impossible. The power of the press is at all times most remarkable, in both domestic and foreign affairs. Not only does it make secrecy in war difficult, but in times of peace it overrides the efforts of diplomacy. Lord John Russell, in his Speeches and Despatches, has put on record how the English press precipitated war between Denmark and Germany on the Schleswig-Holstein dispute. It seems that the British Cabinet had proposed terms of compromise which the German powers were willing to accept; "Denmark," says Lord John Russell, "would likewise have accepted them had not a large portion of the English press, including

the *Times* and *Morning Post*, two powerful organs of
public opinion friendly to the Government, inflamed
the passions of the Danes, and induced them to think
that they would be defended by the arms of England
against even the most moderate demands of Germany,
and against the well-founded complaints of the
oppressed inhabitants of Schleswig. Thus excited,
they refused the proposed terms."

One other point remains, and that is the bearing of
the application of scientific discovery and invention
upon industry and economical questions. And here
we are concerned rather with such inventions as the
machinery employed in the various kinds of manufacture rather than with the railway or telegraph.
Now, the most remarkable and important aspect of
this question is the wonderful way in which the power
of human labour has been multiplied. The power of
producing the means of subsistence has been augmented
enormously. Although population increases, productive power increases much more. The Malthusian
theory is put largely at a discount. A few illustrations
of the multiplication of productive power will do more
for the realization of this important fact than anything
else. The cotton industry may be taken as an example
Sir Lyon Playfair, speaking at the National Liberal
Club on this subject, remarked that "the application
of machinery in the cultivation, harvesting, and clean-
ing of cotton has been so great, that while in 1873 a
given amount of labour produced $3\frac{4}{5}$ million bales in
America, a much less amount of labour in 1887 turned
out $6\frac{1}{2}$ millions of bales. The economies in its manu-

factured products are still greater. In 1873 spindles made four thousand revolutions in a minute; they now make ten thousand. In the last fifteen years the population of the world had increased sixteen per cent., while the production of cotton goods had increased eighty-six per cent." Again, it has been calculated by Professor Leone Levi that if all the yarn which is now spun in England in the course of a year by the machine which spins a thousand threads simultaneously, were to be spun by hand, it would take a hundred millions of men to accomplish the task. Again, it is stated that whereas pig iron can be converted into malleable iron by the Bessemer process in twenty minutes, it formerly took, under the old process, nearly a fortnight to put the iron through the necessary refining and puddling. It becomes apparent, from these instances, that the productive power of human labour has been enormously increased. It seems as though the power of supply had altogether outrun any possible demands. And here, too, the power of rapid locomotion and distribution lend their aid by placing the products of all parts of the world within the reach of all. "A cube of coal," says an American writer, " which would pass through the rim of a quarter of a dollar will drive a ton of food and its proportion of the steamship two miles upon its way from the producer to the consumer." A marvellous achievement! And again says the same writer, "The wages for one day's work of an average mechanic in the far East will pay for moving a year's subsistence of bread and meat a thousand miles or more from the distant West." So

that not only are the products of human labour
enormously increased, but the power of bringing those
products within the reach of all is enormously increased
also.   Nor does the influence of the practical application of science to industry end here.   It has brought
about a revolution in industrial methods, which has
in its turn brought us face to face with social questions
of a most pressing kind.   The relations of capital and
labour, and the life and status of the industrial classes
have been altogether changed by it.   And, indeed, for
the last fifty years the legislators of the world have
been endeavouring to cope with this new order of
things.   The abolition of the corn laws, the introduction of free trade, the various Factory Acts, the
laws affecting trade combinations, the rise of trades
unions, have all had their origin in the difficulties
created by the change.   Scientific discovery has given
birth to an entirely new class of social and political
questions, and if it had done nothing else, it would
have provided questions of great and increasing
interest for the political philosopher and the practical
statesman.

There is a story of an agricultural chemist in South
Carolina, who, shortly before the civil war in America,
was shown the Ordinance of Secession, and was asked
what he thought of it.   He replied, "That's not what
South Carolina needs; she needs manure."   That
chemist expressed by his answer the change that has
come over the world.   He clearly thought that the
practical application of science in South Carolina was
much more important than any question of forms of

government or political institutions. And he was in a great degree right. It may be said that theories and ideas in politics are now forced into the background. Such notions as "the divine right of kings," "social contracts," "natural rights," "rights of man," are of small account. Aristotle, Hobbes, Locke, and Rousseau are, in a sense, no longer the heroes of political philosophy. We are beginning to set up on the thrones which they have vacated, Watt, Arkwright, the Stephensons, and Wheatstone. We do not now so much ask whether this notion or that theory or idea is prevalent in a certain country, but rather what railways it has, whether it has the latest mechanical inventions in manufacture, whether it has many newspapers, and a thorough telegraphic communication at home and with foreign countries. In considering the condition and prospects of a nation, we instinctively feel that such inquiries are more important than an investigation into the political ideas of ·its people. That they should have true and lofty ideas on the great questions that agitate man is well indeed, and likely to redound much to their advantage; but, without the physical and material means to put those ideas into practice, the possession of them is useless, and to talk of them is like the empty tinkling of a cymbal. It is not every one who can proudly say—

> "Content with poverty, my soul I arm,
> And virtue, though in rags, will keep me warm."

The want of physical and material means is an ill school for virtue, and promises but poor nourishment for great ideas and noble thoughts. But the introduction of the railway and the telegraph, and all the other marvels of applied science, lends them powerful aid, and often sweeps away the hidden things of darkness. In politics science is often as beneficent as it is potent.

INDEX.

PRINTED BY WILLIAM CLOWES AND SONS, LIMITED, LONDON AND BECCLES.